THE
Young People's
Pocket
Encyclopedia

Adrienne Jack

KING*f*ISHER

NEW YORK

For Richard and my father Carl L. Norris

KINGFISHER
Larousse Kingfisher Chambers Inc.
95 Madison Avenue
New York, New York 10016

First published in 1998
10 9 8 7 6 5 4 3 2 1

LIBRARY OF CONGRESS CATALOGING-IN-PUBLICATION DATA
    Jack, Adrienne.
        The Kingfisher young people's pocket encyclopedia /
        Jack, Adrienne.
            p.   cm.
        Summary: Presents more than 500 brief alphabetically
        arranged entries on a variety of topics.
        1. Children's encyclopedias and dictionaries. [1.
        Encyclopedias and dictionaries.]   I. Title.
    AG5.J22   1998
    031—dc21   97-47598   CIP AC

ISBN 0-7534-5130-1

Printed in Hong Kong

INTRODUCTION

. . . .

This pocket encyclopedia contains over 500 separate entries. They are arranged in alphabetical order. The information they contain is both interesting and useful.

The encyclopedia can be used in lots of ways. You can look up information on a particular subject for a special project, or you can use it to answer questions that you have been puzzling over, or you can enjoy just browsing through this encyclopedia, stopping when a picture or entry catches your eye.

This is how to look things up:

1. The entries are arranged in *alphabetical order*. Flick through the book until you come to the correct letter for the entry you want to look up.

2. Use the *cross-reference*. "See also" followed by a word or words in capital letters appear at the end of many articles. These words are separate alphabetical entries that will give you more information about your subject.

3. Use the *index*. Sometimes the subject you are looking for may not have a main entry. Look up your subject in the index at the end of the book. The information you need may be contained in an entry with a different title. For instance, information on the Amazon River appears in the articles on Brazil and South America.

A

AARDVARK
The aardvark of Africa is a strange animal. It has no close relatives, although its way of life is like that of the anteater. Aardvarks have strong claws, which they use to break open termites' nests.
   See also ANTEATER.

Aardvark: This timid creature is active mainly at night.

ABORIGINES
Aborigines are the native people of Australia. They arrived there thousands of years ago from Southeast Asia. Traditionally, Aborigines were hunters and foodgatherers, the men hunting emus, kangaroos, and game with

Aborigines: A boomerang and shield with traditional decorations.

boomerangs and spears, the women gathering nuts, berries, and fruits. This way of life has changed, as today many live and work in the cities or on large farms.

ACID
Acids are sour-tasting chemicals. The sour taste of a lemon is caused by citric acid. Sour milk contains lactic acid. Vinegar contains acetic acid. These are weak acids and are harmless. Strong acids, such as sulfuric acid, nitric acid, and hydrochloric acid, are poisonous.

AFRICA
Africa is the world's second-largest continent. Most of the land is a great plateau, or tableland, surrounded by a narrow coastal plain. In the east are volcanic mountains such as Mount Kilimanjaro (19,340 feet high) and Mount Kenya (17,060 feet high).

Africa: The high plains of Africa are home to a great variety of wildlife.

The equator falls near the middle of Africa. The climate near the equator is hot and wet. Great rain forests grow here. On either side of the equator there are vast savannas. These grasslands are dry for most of the year. Beyond these are areas of scrub, then semidesert, and then desert. The Sahara is in the north and the Kalahari in the south.

Much of Africa is thinly populated. Cocoa, coffee, oil palm, tea, tobacco, cotton, and sugar are grown to sell to countries all over the world. The continent is also rich in minerals.

See also COUNTRIES OF THE WORLD; EGYPT; NIGERIA; SOUTH AFRICA.

AIDS

AIDS stands for "acquired immune deficiency syndrome," a deadly disease caused by a virus. The virus itself is called the human immunodeficiency virus, or HIV for short. The disease slowly cripples the body's immune system, leaving the victim with no defense at all against infection. In the early 1980s, AIDS spread rapidly from developing countries all through the Western world. It is passed on mainly through sexual contact and exchanges of infected blood. A cure is still not in sight.

AIR

Air is the substance that fills the "empty" space around us. It is made up of a mixture of gases, the main ones being nitrogen and oxygen.

Aircraft: Military jet aircraft have a streamlined shape to help them fly at supersonic speeds.

Oxygen is the gas animals must breathe in order to live. Air is invisible and has no taste, but when it moves we can feel it as wind. Water vapor, another invisible substance, is also in the air.

A layer of air, called the atmosphere, surrounds the Earth. The air in the atmosphere presses down on us. This is called atmospheric pressure.

AIRCRAFT

Two American brothers built and flew the first airplane in 1903. They were Wilbur and Orville Wright from Dayton, Ohio. Their first flimsy flying machine was made from wood, cloth, and wire. It could fly only a few feet and could not travel much faster than a bicycle.

Modern planes are very different from the Wright brothers' flying machine. They are sleek and streamlined and made from aluminum alloys. With their powerful jet engines they can travel at fantastic speeds.

There are many different types of planes, but, whatever they are like, all planes have certain things in common. They all have wings shaped to enable them to fly. The shape is called an airfoil, and consists of a thickened and rounded front edge, curving and tapering to a sharper rear edge. All planes have a tail, which helps to keep the plane on a straight course.

To guide a plane through the air a pilot moves hinged panels, called control surfaces, at the rear of the wings and on the tail. By moving these surfaces, the pilot can make the plane's nose tip up or down or turn to the left or right. Many planes today are flown with the help of electronics and computers.

Planes are thrust through the air either by a stream, or jet, of gases or by propellers. In a jet engine fuel is burned to make hot gases. These gases shoot backward, pushing the plane forward. Propellers have a twisted shape and "screw" themselves through the air when they spin.

See also BALLOON AND AIRSHIP; BLÉRIOT; HELICOPTER; JET ENGINE; LINDBERGH; WRIGHT.

AIR-CUSHION VEHICLE
See HOVERCRAFT.

ALEXANDER THE GREAT
(356–323 B.C.)
Alexander was king of Macedonia in Greece and a mighty conqueror. His great dream was to conquer the whole world. He subdued his Greek neighbors in 336 B.C. By 327 B.C. he had conquered the huge Persian Empire to the east. He then led his men into India, but they were exhausted and he turned back. When he reached Babylon he died of a fever aged 33.

ALGAE
Algae are the simplest plants. They live where there is moisture. Seaweed is a common alga. Another is the green slime that covers the sides of an aquarium.

Like all plants, algae use the energy in sunlight to make their food. They are food themselves for many water animals, including shellfish and even whales.

There are four kinds of algae. Green algae live near the surface. Lower down live the blue-green, brown, and red algae.
See also PLANT.

Algae: Algae take many forms, but none have true roots and stems.

Kelp

Cockscomb   Bladder wrack   Red rags

7

ALLOY

When two metals are mixed, the result is an alloy. Copper and zinc form the alloy brass. The most common alloy is steel, a mixture of iron and carbon, often with other substances added. Alloys are often used instead of pure metals because they are stronger.

ALPHABET

An alphabet is a group of letters, or signs, that stand for sounds. It is used to write a language.

The English alphabet comes from the Roman alphabet. It has 26 letters. The letters of the Greek alphabet are used as signs by scientists. The first two Greek letters, *alpha* (A) and *beta* (B), give us the word "alphabet."

ALUMINUM

Aluminum is the most important metal, after iron. It is light, does not rust, and can be made into strong alloys, so it is used in the building of aircraft and ships. It conducts heat well and is often used to make pots and pans.

See also ALLOY; METAL.

AMPHIBIAN

Amphibians were the first prehistoric animals to adapt to life on dry land. Modern amphibians —cold-blooded animals such as frogs, toads, salamanders, and newts, still spend part of their lives in water and part on dry land.

All amphibians have backbones, and nearly all lay their eggs in water. The young breathe through gills. Adults develop lungs and can leave the water. Amphibians absorb water through their skins, so they must keep themselves moist all the time.

Anglo-Saxon: *An Anglo-Saxon helmet decorated with gold.*

ANGLO-SAXON

Anglo-Saxons—the Angles, Saxons, and Jutes—were people from Germany who settled in Britain in the 5th and 6th centuries, driving the original Celtic people into Wales and Cornwall. The Anglo-Saxons ruled Britain until the Norman Conquest in 1066.

ANIMAL

There are two groups of living things on Earth, animals and plants.

Unlike most plants, most animals can move around. Many have senses, such as sight, hearing, and smell, along with a nervous system and a brain. Senses help their owner to find food and escape enemies. Animals use the oxygen they breathe to burn food, which gives them the energy they need. The simplest animals, such as the amoeba, consist of one cell. Other animals are made up of different types of cells joined together.

The animal kingdom is divided into two groups. The larger is the invertebrate group. This includes animals without a backbone, such as insects, worms, crabs, spiders, snails, and starfish.

Animals with backbones are called vertebrates. They include fish, amphibians, reptiles, birds, and mammals. Most mammals give birth to live young. Almost all others lay eggs.

All animals behave in certain ways at certain times. This automatic behavior, such as nest-building, migrating, or attacking prey, is called instinct. Invertebrates almost always act instinctively. Vertebrates have more complex brains and can learn. Most animals can send each other simple messages.

See also BRAIN; CAMOUFLAGE; CELL; EVOLUTION; MIGRATION, ANIMAL; REPRODUCTION; SENSES.

Use the Index to look up animals and animal groups.

ANT

Ants are called social insects because they live in large colonies. There may be as many as a million ants in one nest.

There are three kinds of ants in a colony—a queen, workers, and males. The queen mates with a

Ant: Eggs, larvae, and pupae are taken care of by workers in a series of chambers inside the nest.

winged male and spends her whole life laying eggs. The female workers cannot lay eggs. They look after the nest, collect food, and care for the young. The males mate with the queen.

Ants live in all but the coldest parts of the world. Some have interesting habits. The umbrella ants chew up leaves and use them for growing food. Army ants march in vast columns and eat any living thing in their path.

ANTARCTICA

Antarctica is covered with a sheet of ice thousands of feet thick. It is colder than the Arctic. Even in summer, the temperature rarely rises above freezing point. The South Pole is near the center of a high, windswept plain.

Algae, mosses and lichens, and some tiny insects live on the continent. The surrounding sea is rich in plankton, fish, seals, and whales, and penguins and other birds are also found there.

ANTEATER

The anteater lives in the forests and savanna of Central and South America. It has a tubular snout and a long, sticky tongue. It feeds on ants and termites, breaking open their nests with its powerful claws.

ANTELOPE

The graceful antelope are related to cattle. They run swiftly on two-toed hooves and, like cows, chew the cud.

There are antelope in Africa and Asia. Most live in herds on grassy plains, but some kinds prefer forests or marshes.

See also CATTLE.

ANTIBIOTIC

Antibiotics are drugs that either kill bacteria or stop them from spreading. Doctors use them to treat diseases such as pneumonia and tuberculosis that are caused by bacteria. Commonly used antibiotics include penicillin and tetracycline. Many antibiotics, such as penicillin, come from mold; others, such as tetracycline, are produced by bacteria found in the soil.

See also BACTERIA; DISEASE; DRUGS.

Anteater: The anteater uses its long snout to reach inside insects' nests.

APE

Apes include gorillas, chimpanzees, gibbons, and orangutans. They are the animals most like humans, with the same number of teeth and the same kind of skeleton. They also have the same kind of blood and catch many similar diseases.

After humans, apes are the most intelligent of all animals. Even so, an ape's brain is only half the size of a human's. Young apes are playful and easily tamed. Apes use their hands and feet skillfully and can solve simple problems.

Unlike monkeys, apes don't have tails. Sometimes they stand erect, but usually they move around on all fours, walking on the knuckles of their hands.

Ape: *Apes such as this gorilla live in tropical forests and mainly eat leaves, fruit, nuts, and insects.*

ARCHAEOLOGY

Archaeology is the study of how people lived long ago through the clues they left behind—their buildings, weapons, ornaments, coins, bones, and tools. These clues are often buried underground.

Archaeologists excavate, or dig out, buried finds. The deeper they dig, the older the objects they find. From human bones, broken pots, kitchen garbage, and other remains they can learn how the people lived, what foods they ate, and what skills they had. As a site is excavated, each find is cleaned, labeled, and handled with great care as it can be very fragile.

Archaeologists can tell the age of an object in several ways. They study the soil and other remains found near it. They can date a find by measuring the amount of natural radioactivity left in certain objects—the carbon-14 method—or by counting the number of tree rings—dendrochronology.

Archaeologists are not just interested in ancient civilization and buried sites. Some, known as industrial archaeologists, study old factories and machinery.

ARCHERY

The use of bows and arrows is called archery. Prehistoric men used bows for hunting and in battle. In the Middle Ages, English archers were famous for their skill with the longbow, which had a

Archery: A longbow in action.

longer range than the more complicated crossbow. Bows and arrows became out-of-date when guns were invented. Today archery is a sport.

ARCHIMEDES (*c.*287–212 B.C.)

The Greek mathematician, Archimedes, lived in Sicily. He discovered that the volume of an object can be measured by the amount of water that it displaces. He also invented Archimedes' screw for lifting water.

ARCHITECTURE

Architecture is the art and science of designing buildings. The architect draws up the plans that construction workers follow. Many styles of architecture have been used through the ages. Architecture tells the story of how civilizations grow.

The Greeks tried to be perfect in everything they did. Their system of building was very simple. Rows of tall marble columns supported stone beams,

Architecture: The world's skyscrapers include the Empire State Building (left), the World Trade Center (center), and the Sears Tower (right).

Architecture: Ulm Cathedral in Germany was built in the 19th century, but its style is Gothic.

Small stones and cement could be used instead of heavy marble beams.

In Europe during the Middle Ages, stone was the natural material for building strong castles and long-lasting cathedrals. At first, architects followed Roman styles. This is called Romanesque architecture. But from around 1150 they began building tall, slender churches and cathedrals, using pointed arches instead of round ones. This is called the Gothic style.

During the Renaissance, architects returned to the Greek and Roman styles. They liked the simple "classical" designs.

PERIODS OF ARCHITECTURE

B.C.

3200s	Ancient Egyptian begins
600s	Classical Greek begins
100s	Classical Roman begins

A.D.

400s	Byzantine period begins
950s	Romanesque period in northern Europe
1000s	Norman period in England
1150s	Gothic period begins in France
1400s	Renaissance period in Italy
1600s	Baroque period begins in Italy
1720s	Georgian style begins in England
1750s	Rococo style begins in Italy
1890s	Art nouveau in Europe
1920s	Modern architecture begins with functionalism and the International Style

onto which the roof was placed.

Greek architecture was copied later by the Romans. But the Roman architects added two important developments: the arch and the vault, a roof supported by arches. The arch was a good way to span a wide distance quickly.

13

They gradually added more decoration until, by the 1600s, buildings had become very ornate, inside and outside. Even straight stone columns were twisted into spiral shapes. This was called the baroque style.

An important development in the 1900s was the introduction of steel and reinforced concrete. These materials allowed architects to build more quickly and much higher than before. The first very tall buildings, called "skyscrapers" were built in the United States. Now they are built all over the world.

Today's architects use simple shapes. The architect tries to design a new building so that it will fit in well with other buildings near it.

See also CASTLE; CHURCH; EGYPT, ANCIENT; GREECE, ANCIENT; ROME, ANCIENT.

ARCTIC

The Arctic is the cold frozen zone around the North Pole. At the North Pole the Sun never rises in winter. In summer the Sun does not set, even at midnight.

The Arctic Ocean includes both the frozen sea around the North Pole and the unfrozen waters surrounding that. Because so many rivers flow into it from northern Europe, Asia, and North America, it is less salty than the world's other oceans.

During the short Arctic summer, grass, flowers, and moss grow on the tundra plains of the Arctic. Arctic animals include seals, walruses, whales, polar bears, foxes, owls, weasels, musk oxen, and reindeer. The only people native to the Arctic are the Inuit. There are many minerals in the Arctic, including coal, oil, and iron.

ARGENTINA

Argentina is the second-largest country in South America. It is a land of farms and ranches, and from these come many different products. Rice, sugarcane, and other tropical crops are grown in the north of the country. Cattle and grain come from the central plains, or pampas. Grapes and other fruit are farmed in the west, and fruit and sheep in the cold, dry south.

Argentina was ruled by Spain from 1516 to 1810. In 1966, military leaders took control of the government. In 1982, Argentina and Britain fought a war over the ownership of the Falkland Islands.

See also PAGE 62.

ARISTOTLE (384–322 B.C.)

Aristotle was a Greek philosopher who invented the method of thinking called logic. A student of Plato, Aristotle became tutor to

Armor: *Plate armor, designed for medieval knights on horseback, could be very ornate.*

Alexander the Great. His writings cover many subjects, including politics and nature.

ARMADILLO

This South American mammal looks a lot like a small pig, but it is armored like a tank. It is a timid animal and rolls itself into a ball when frightened. Armadillos eat worms, insects, and roots. They use their strong claws to search for food and to dig out burrows.

ARMOR

Before gunpowder was invented, soldiers fought in hand-to-hand combat. To protect their bodies, they wore armor. Leather made good, light armor and could be made stronger by adding plates of bronze or iron. The Greeks and Romans wore helmets, leg armor and breastplates.

Later armorers learned to link tiny iron rings together to make coats of mail. Mail gave good protection against swords and spears, but steel plate was even stronger. Plate armor covered the whole of a man's body. But even steel armor was no defense against the cannon. By the 1600s soldiers needed to move more quickly, so they wore less armor.

ART

See PAINTING; SCULPTURE.

ASIA

Asia is the largest continent (17,135,000 sq. mi.). It stretches from the Arctic to the equator and from Japan in the east to the Middle East and Russia in the west. It contains 48 separate countries and its population of

3.5 billion is over half the world's total population.

There are many different types of land and climate in Asia. In the north are evergreen forests, flat grasslands called steppes, and cold tundra plains. In central Asia are the world's highest mountains, including the Himalayas. Some of the world's longest rivers flow across the continent.

Almost all of Asia's people live either in the fertile river valleys or on the coastal plains. Most of them are farmers, scraping a living out of a small patch of land, but more and more people are going to live in the cities.

Rice is the main crop of the warm, wet monsoon lands of southern Asia. Rice and fish are the main foods of many Asians. Other crops are tea, sugar, cotton, coffee, and spices.

Asia has many valuable raw materials. The forests provide timber and rubber. There are minerals such as coal, iron, copper, and tin. In the Middle East there is oil beneath the desert. The most important industrial country in Asia is Japan, which manufactures many products to sell to other countries. China, Korea, and India are also developing rapidly.

Asia has a long history of rich and powerful civilizations. The great religions of Christianity, Islam, Hinduism, and Buddhism all began in Asia. Asian peoples reached high levels of progress in the arts and sciences long before the rest of the world.

European explorers came to Asia in the 1400s in search of riches and spices. They set up trading stations, and later founded colonies. Today, all the countries of Asia are independent.

See also CHINA; COUNTRIES OF THE WORLD; INDIA; JAPAN; MIDDLE EAST.

ASTRONAUT

An astronaut is a person who travels in space. People had been dreaming of doing this for thousands of years, but it was not until April 1961 that the first person in space orbited the Earth. This was the Russian cosmonaut, Yuri Gagarin. In July 1969, the American, Neil Armstrong, was the first person to set foot on the Moon.

Traveling in space is one of the most exciting and dangerous things people have ever done. The astronauts have to be well trained before they can go. For example, they must learn to withstand the great force caused by the rocket thrust, and to eat, move, and sleep in weightless conditions.

In space there is no air to breathe, so astronauts take a supply of air in their spacecraft. To walk in space they wear a space suit. This supplies them

Helmet

Camera

In-suit drink bag

Temperature control valve

NASA

Computer display

15 layers of plastic

Cooling fluid inside space suit

Boots

Astronaut: Many controls are built into an astronaut's space suit.

with air and keeps their bodies at the right temperature.

See also GRAVITY; SPACE EXPLORATION.

ASTRONOMY

Astronomy is the study of the stars, planets, and other objects in the universe. People first began to record what they observed in the sky in ancient times. They used these records to predict events such as eclipses. Later, records of this kind were used to figure out, check, and correct calendars.

Astronomers now work with a variety of instruments in well-equipped observatories. Their most useful instrument is the telescope, which gathers and strengthens the feeble light reaching us from the stars. In recent years astronomers have learned much from information collected by spacecraft.

See also COMET; CONSTELLATION; COPERNICUS; GALILEO; METEOR; STAR; TELESCOPE; UNIVERSE.

ATHLETICS

The sport of athletics began with the exercises used to train men for battle. The ancient Greeks loved athletics, and at the Olympic Games young men competed with each other at running, wrestling, and throwing.

The modern athlete must train hard to do well. In an athletics event today there are running, or track events; and jumping and throwing, or field events.

ATLANTIC OCEAN

Second only in size to the Pacific, the Atlantic Ocean covers an area of more than 30,000,000 sq. mi. and includes many gulfs and seas. Islands include Greenland,

Iceland, the British Isles, the West Indies, the Azores, and the Falkland Islands. On the ocean floor are tall underwater mountains, including the Mid-Atlantic Ridge, a mountain chain running from Iceland almost to the tip of South America. Atlantic currents include the Gulf Stream, which warms northern Europe, and the Brazil Current.

ATOM

Every substance is a combination of one or more chemical elements. Iron is an element. If you could cut a piece of iron into smaller and smaller pieces, eventually you would be left with tiny particles called atoms. They are the smallest particles of an element that can exist.

At the center of the atom is a nucleus. This contains two kinds of particles, called protons and neutrons. The protons have a positive electric charge. Circling the nucleus are tiny particles, called electrons. These have a negative electric charge.

Every element is made of a different kind of atom. Atoms of different elements combine to form molecules of a new substance. Two atoms of hydrogen (H) combine with one atom of oxygen (O) to form one molecule of water. We can therefore represent water like this: H_2O.

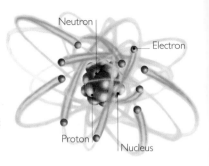

Atom: An atom is held together by the electrical attraction between protons in the nucleus and electrons circling around the nucleus.

AUSTRALIA

Australia is the largest island in the world and the smallest continent. Low mountains run all the way down the east coast. Most of the center is grassy plain, and the western part consists of flat scrubland, barren, rolling hills, and desert. About four-fifths of the continent is hot desert.

Along the northeastern coast is a chain of beautifully-colored coral reefs, islands, and sandbanks called the Great Barrier Reef. Most people have settled in the southeast, where there is enough water available.

The seasons are the exact opposite of those in the Northern Hemisphere. When it is spring in the United States, it is fall in Australia. Winters are mild and there is plenty of sunshine.

Although the Dutch "discovered" Australia in 1606, they did not settle it. Captain Cook claimed eastern Australia for Britain in 1770. In 1788, 800 convicts were sent to Botany Bay, and became Australia's earliest colonists.

Australia is a farming country. It produces wool, dairy foods, meat, fruit, and wheat to sell to the rest of the world. Australia mines valuable minerals, too. They include gold, silver, coal, lead, copper, tin, and uranium.

It is also the home of many strange plants and animals, such as the platypus and emu, which are found nowhere else in the world.

Aztec: Aztec temples had a chamber at the top where the priests worshiped animal gods and made sacrifices.

Many of the native animals are marsupials—animals that carry their young around in pouches until they are old enough to take care of themselves. These include the kangaroo, koala, and wombat.

See also ABORIGINES; KANGAROO; KOALA; PLATYPUS; PAGE 63.

AUSTRIA
See SWITZERLAND AND AUSTRIA.

AUTOMOBILE
See CAR.

AZTEC
The Aztecs were an ancient people who lived in Mexico. Their great city, Tenochtitlán, had huge temple pyramids. The city was built on an island in an area of many lakes, so people traveled around in boats. When the Spanish explorer Cortés entered Mexico in 1519, he was astonished to find such a civilization.

The Spaniards wanted the Aztecs' gold, of which they had a very large quantity. Although their army was small, the Spaniards had guns and horses, and were able to conquer the Aztecs easily.

B

BACH, JOHANN SEBASTIAN (1685–1750)
J. S. Bach is the most famous of the great German composers and musicians. He was a master of the organ and composed hundreds of pieces of music, including many choral works.

BACTERIA
Bacteria are among the smallest living things. Each one is made up of just a single cell, and can only be seen under a microscope. There are millions of bacteria all around us.

Some bacteria feed on dead creatures and waste, causing them to decay. They make the soil rich and help plants to grow. Bacteria also turn meat rotten and milk sour; some cause disease.

BADGER
The badger is a relative of the weasel. It is a powerfully built animal with short legs and a black-and-white striped head.

Badgers dig deep burrows called sets, and emerge from them after dark to find food. They will fight fiercely if attacked but, when they are left alone, they are peaceful animals.

BALLET
See DANCE.

BALLOON AND AIRSHIP
Balloons and airships use gases such as helium, hydrogen, and hot air to fly. These gases are lighter than air. While balloons can only drift in the wind, airships can be flown with precision.

The first balloon to carry people was built by the Montgolfier brothers in 1783. A fire was built beneath an open-ended bag, filling it with hot air.

Today balloons are used by

Badger: These woodland animals feed on a mixture of plants, insects, and small mammals.

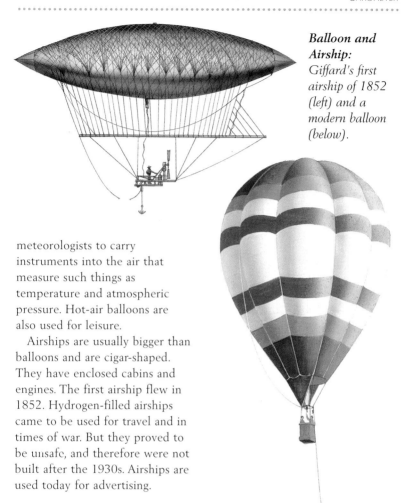

Balloon and Airship: *Giffard's first airship of 1852 (left) and a modern balloon (below).*

meteorologists to carry instruments into the air that measure such things as temperature and atmospheric pressure. Hot-air balloons are also used for leisure.

Airships are usually bigger than balloons and are cigar-shaped. They have enclosed cabins and engines. The first airship flew in 1852. Hydrogen-filled airships came to be used for travel and in times of war. But they proved to be unsafe, and therefore were not built after the 1930s. Airships are used today for advertising.

BAROMETER

A barometer is an instrument used to measure air pressure. It can help forecast the weather and measure height above sea level.

There are two major types of barometer: the mercury and the aneroid. The aneroid barometer is more commonly used. It has a

drum from which most of the air has been removed. When the air pressure outside the drum changes, the size of the drum changes. This change in size is recorded on a scale.

If a barometer shows high pressure, it means good weather.

21

BASEBALL

Baseball is the national American sport. It may have come from an English game called rounders. Two teams of nine players each take turns to bat the ball and score runs around the baseball diamond. The national championships are played in the World Series, held each October.

BASKETBALL

Basketball is played on a court by two teams of five players each. Points are made by throwing a ball through a basket. Each

Baseball: The hard leather ball is hit with a cylindrical bat.

"basket" counts as two points. Free throws, for fouls, count as one point. It helps to be tall in this game.

BAT

Bats are the only mammals that can fly. Their large wings consist of thin skin stretched between the fingers of the forelimb and the hindlimb. They sleep by day, hanging upside down in caves or other dark places. Insect-eating bats cannot see well, yet they can fly in the dark without bumping into obstacles.

Bat: Bats unfold their powerful wings in order to fly. Their large ears help them pick up echoes from obstacles.

To do this they send out very high-pitched squeaks and listen for the echo that bounces off the things around them.

The vampire bat of South America feeds on the blood of other animals. The largest bats are fruit eaters.

BEAR

Although bears may look cuddly and playful, they are dangerous animals. They are very strong and have sharp claws. Although some bears can be tamed, they may still attack without warning.

Bears live mainly in forests and mountains. They are meat eaters, but they also eat most kinds of plants and fish. Some bears hibernate (sleep) during the winter, living on fat stored in their bodies.

There are several different kinds of bears. The largest—the grizzly, the Kodiak, and the polar—are from North America. The polar bear also lives in northern Europe. The sun bear, from Asia, is the smallest.

BEAVER

These rodents have stout bodies and short legs. Their webbed feet and paddlelike tails make them good swimmers. They can stay underwater for several minutes.

Beavers live in family groups. They make a home safe from enemies by damming streams and small rivers with branches, stones, and mud. In the pool formed behind the dam, the beavers build their lodge, a dome-shaped den of mud and sticks with an underwater entrance.

BEE AND WASP

Bees are very useful insects. They make honey and wax. More importantly, by pollinating plants bees help them produce seeds.

Some types of bees are solitary. Others, such as the bumblebee and the honeybee, are social insects and live in large colonies. Social insects build a nest or hive. In every beehive there are many worker bees, a few male drones, and a queen.

Bee and Wasp: *Bees use the honeycomb cells inside the hive to store food and house larvae.*

Bee and Wasp: Worker bees collect pollen in sacs on their legs.

After mating with a drone, the queen bee starts to lay thousands of eggs. The workers are small female bees. They build the wax cells of the comb and gather nectar and pollen from flowers to store inside. Workers also feed the queen and the larvae and guard the hive. Drones do not work, and in the fall they are driven from the hive to die.

Wasps are related to bees, and are hunting insects. Social wasps, like social bees, live in colonies with a queen, drones, and workers. Adult wasps eat nectar, but the larvae are fed on insects and caterpillars. In the fall all the wasps die, except for the young queens. They hibernate through the winter and start new nests in the spring. Solitary wasps live alone and build small nests.

See also INSECT.

BEETHOVEN, LUDWIG VAN (1770–1827)

Beethoven was a German composer who wrote some of the world's greatest music. He started writing music when he was a boy. In later life he went deaf, but still continued to write music.

See also MUSIC.

BELGIUM

See NETHERLANDS, BELGIUM, AND LUXEMBOURG.

BELL, ALEXANDER GRAHAM (1847–1922)

This Scottish-born teacher of the deaf is best remembered as the inventor of the telephone. On March 10, 1876, Bell spoke the

Bell: Bell's telephone used weak electric charges traveling down a wire to transmit sounds.

historic first message over the telephone to his assistant: "Mr. Watson, come here; I want you."

BIBLE

The Bible is in two parts—the Old and New Testaments. It was written at different times and by different people, but most of it is thousands of years old.

The Old Testament is held sacred by Jews and Christians. It tells the stories of the Jewish people, their kings, and their prophets. The New Testament is sacred only to Christians. It contains the four gospels of Matthew, Mark, Luke, and John.

Gospel means "good news." Each of these "evangelists" tells the story of Jesus' life: his birth in Bethlehem, his teaching, his death on the cross, and his resurrection. See also CHRISTIANITY; JESUS CHRIST.

BICYCLE

The first bicycle was built around 1790 by a Frenchman named De Sivrac. Early bicycles were steered by the front wheel and propelled by the rider pushing his feet on the ground. Later bicycles had pedals to propel them. The famous "penny farthing" bicycle had the pedals attached to its huge front wheel. More and more improvements were made until, by the end of the 1800s, bicycles resembled today's models.

The modern bicycle is propelled

Bicycle: A modern touring bicycle (above) and a "penny farthing" from the 1880s (right).

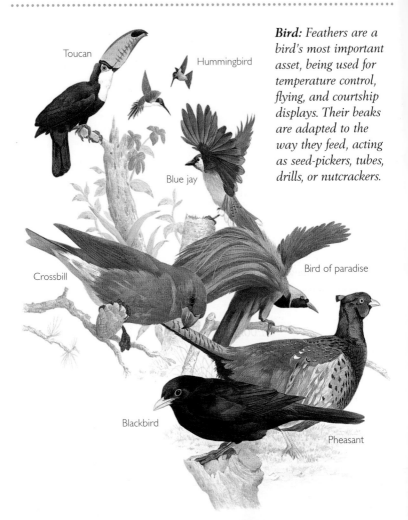

Toucan

Hummingbird

Bird: *Feathers are a bird's most important asset, being used for temperature control, flying, and courtship displays. Their beaks are adapted to the way they feed, acting as seed-pickers, tubes, drills, or nutcrackers.*

Blue jay

Crossbill

Bird of paradise

Blackbird

Pheasant

by pedals attached to cranks. The cranks turn a toothed wheel which turns a chain which drives the rear wheel.

BIOLOGY

Biology is the study of living things—their structure, their development, and their relationship to other living things. Within the wide field of biology are many specialized sciences, such as botany (the study of plants), zoology (the study of animals), cytology (the study of cells), genetics (the study of

Title: _Pocket Ency._

Au: _KingFisher_

BD DISTRIBUTOES

ISBN: - _51301_

QTY: _1_

LIST PRICE: _10.95_   6/00/05

#_____ AS OF _/_ _/05_

heredity), anatomy (the study of the structures of plants and animals), bacteriology (the study of bacteria), and paleontology (the study of fossils). Ecologists study the relationship of plants and animals to their environments.

In recent years, space biology has been added to the list. Scientists in this field study what happens to living things when they are taken into space.

BIRD

All birds have wings, though some cannot fly. They have feathers, and beaks instead of jaws.

Most birds are perfectly built for flight. Their bones are hollow and light, but strong. Their wing muscles are powerful. Their feathers help them fly, and also keep them warm and dry.

Birds rely mostly on eyesight to find food, but their taste and hearing are also good. They are born with the skills they need. Much of their behavior is not learned but comes from instinct.

Birds reproduce by laying eggs. In order to hatch, the eggs must be kept warm, so parent birds sit on them. When the young hatch, they are helpless and must be fed.

See also EAGLE; HUMMINGBIRD; KIWI; OWL; PENGUIN.

BISON

Bison are wild cattle. They are large, powerful animals with humped shoulders, thick fur, and short horns.

The North American bison is sometimes called the buffalo. Vast

Bison: *The North American bison is a protected species.*

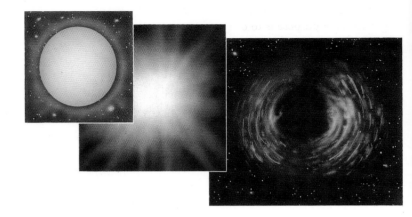

herds provided food for the Native Americans, but European settlers killed so many that the animal almost died out. The European bison, or wisent, is also rare.

Black hole: *At the end of its life a massive star explodes (center) and then collapses. The resulting gravitational pull draws in everything around, even light(right).*

BLACK HOLE

When a star begins to lose its ability to produce energy, it starts a slow process of collapsing in on itself. If the collapsing star is very big it explodes, and the remaining atoms become densely packed together as it collapses. The electrons and protons in the atoms combine to become neutrons, and the star is called a neutron star.

If even the neutrons are crushed by gravity, the gravitational force created at the center is so strong that everything in its gravitational field is drawn inward. It is called a black hole because even light cannot escape.

See also STAR.

BLÉRIOT, LOUIS (1872–1936)

Blériot, a Frenchman, was one of the great pilots in the history of flying. In 1909, a British newspaper offered a prize to the first person to fly the English Channel. Blériot accepted this challenge and flew the 25 miles from Calais, France, to Dover, England, in 37 minutes. He continued to design and later to manufacture airplanes.

BLOOD

Blood is made of red and white cells, and platelets, that all float in a watery liquid called plasma. Blood is pumped around the body by the heart. There are around ten pints in an average adult.

Blood does several important things. Its main purpose is to carry substances around the body. It takes oxygen from the lungs and nutrients from the intestines and distributes them to body cells. It takes waste products from the cells to the lungs and kidneys. Blood also carries heat around the body from the muscles where most heat is produced.

Finally, blood protects the body. The platelets help the blood to clot when the skin is wounded. The white cells fight infection by attacking germs, and can produce substances to counteract poisons produced by the germs.

See also HEART.

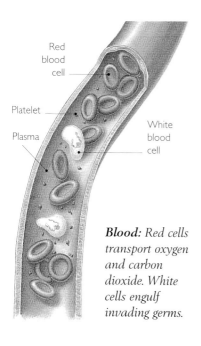

Blood: *Red cells transport oxygen and carbon dioxide. White cells engulf invading germs.*

Red blood cell

Platelet

Plasma

White blood cell

BOADICEA
(DIED A.D. 60)
Boadicea (or Boudicca) was queen of the Iceni tribe during the Roman occupation of Britain. When the Romans seized Iceni property and treated them badly, Boadicea and the Iceni rebelled. Many Britons joined them. When they were finally defeated, Boadicea poisoned herself.

BOLÍVAR, SIMÓN (1783–1830)
When Bolívar was born, most of South America was ruled by Spain. "The Liberator," as he is often known, led the fight for freedom. He headed the armies that drove the Spanish from the northern part of the continent, winning a great victory at the Battle of Boyacá in 1819. Later he helped to drive the Spanish from Peru. At the time he was the most powerful man in South America. The present-day country of Bolivia was named after him.

BONE
Bones make up the framework or skeleton of all vertebrates (animals with backbones). They are very strong. Two-thirds of a bone is mineral, which makes it hard. One-third is animal matter, which makes it difficult to break.

Bones have several functions. They protect important organs such as the brain, heart, and lungs, and support the limbs. Some bones are hollow and filled with a red substance called marrow. Marrow makes the red and white cells of the blood.

All bones have names, such as scapula (shoulder blade), patella (kneecap), and skull. There are 206 bones in the human body.

BOOK

Books are one of the most important inventions. All that we know, and all the ideas, thoughts, beliefs, and literature of the past can be found in books. We use them to learn from, for amusement, and for inspiration.

The earliest-known books were written by the Egyptians in about 2500 B.C. They were written on paper made from reeds and were rolled up to form a scroll. The Romans were the first to make modern-looking books. They were inscribed by hand on parchment or vellum made from animal skin.

In 1439, when Johannes Gutenberg invented his printing machine, movable type began to be used and more than one book could be printed at a time.

See also GUTENBERG; PAPER.

BOXING

Boxing is the ancient sport of fighting with the fists. Today the boxers wear gloves, and the matches are divided into three-minute rounds. Boxers are classed by weight. They follow rules set out by an English nobleman in 1872.

BRAHMS, JOHANNES (1833–1897)

This great German composer wrote songs, dances, concertos, and symphonies. His *German Requiem* is one of the world's great works for chorus and orchestra. Brahms was a lifelong friend of Robert Schumann, the romantic composer.

BRAILLE

Braille is a form of writing used by blind people. A braille book has raised dots on its page instead of printed letters. By touching the dots with their fingertips, blind people can read. They can also type in braille, using a machine that stamps out the dots through the paper. The braille alphabet was invented by a Frenchman called Louis Braille. He lived from 1809 to 1852, and was blind from the age of three.

BRAIN

The brain and its extension, the spinal cord, are called the central nervous system.

The brain is divided into several different parts, each with its own job. One part, the medulla oblongata, controls breathing, heart-rate, and digestion, all of

A· B: C·· D·: E·.
F·· G:: H:· I·· J·:
K: L:· M:· N:· O:·
P:· Q:: R:· S:· T·:
U:. V:. W·: X:: Y::
Z::

and	for	of	the
::	::	::	..

with	fraction	numeral	poetry	apostrophe
::	·	·:	·:	·

hyphen	dash	comma	semicolon	colon
··	·· ··	·	:	··

Braille: *Patterns of raised dots represent letters and can be arranged into words and sentences.*

which you do without thinking. The hypo-thalamus controls the body's temperature and governs involuntary drives such as hunger and thirst. The cerebellum controls muscular coordination and balance.

The largest part of the brain is the cerebral cortex. Different parts of the body are linked to different areas of the cortex. The senses—sight, hearing, and

Brain: *The cerebral cortex fills most of the skull. Activities such as vision, hearing, and movement have specific areas within it. It also deals with personality and intelligence.*

touch—have their own areas, as do memory, thought, movement, and language.

The spinal cord receives messages from the nerves and carries them to the brain. It also carries messages from the brain to the nerves in all parts of the body to make them work.

BRAZIL

This is the largest country in South America. It covers 3,285,000 sq. mi. The equator crosses the north of Brazil. Just south of the equator the mighty Amazon River flows from the Andes to the Atlantic.

The Amazon valley is a vast area of tropical plants and animals.

Cerebral cortex

Medulla oblongata

Cerebellum

Spinal cord

31

Today many of the trees are being cut down, destroying this important natural area.

Most of Brazil's 162 million people live in cities. It is the world's largest producer of coffee. Beef, cocoa, maize, sugarcane, and tobacco are also produced. Oil has been discovered and there are many industries.

The Portuguese ruled Brazil from 1500 to 1825. It became a republic in 1889.

See also PAGE 62.

BREATHING

All animals breathe. They need oxygen from the air in order to burn the food they eat and make energy from it.

Humans breathe through lungs. Lungs are spongy bags inside the body that fill with air when we breathe in. Oxygen from the air goes into the blood, and we breathe out carbon dioxide.

Fish breathe through gills, which trap the oxygen dissolved in water. Insects breathe through tiny holes in the hard outer casing of their bodies.

BRIDGE

There are three basic types of bridge—girder, arch, and suspension. These types can be combined in many ways and can be made from wood, stone, bricks, iron, concrete, or steel.

The kind of bridge used for a site depends upon three factors: the hardness of the ground, the width and depth of the valley or river to be spanned, and the weight to be carried.

The Romans built marvelous arch bridges, some of which still stand. Coalbrookdale, the first iron bridge, is an arch bridge. It was built in Britain in 1779.

The first major suspension bridge was the Menai Bridge in Wales, in Britain, built by Thomas Telford in 1826. The suspension bridge with the longest span is the Akashi-Kaikyo bridge between the Honshu and Awaji islands in Japan.

BRITISH ISLES

There are about 5,000 islands in the British Isles, the largest of which are Great Britain and Ireland. Great Britain consists of England, Scotland, and Wales, which together form the United Kingdom. Northern Ireland is also governed by the United Kingdom, but most of Ireland is an independent republic. The climate of the British Isles is mild, with heavier rainfall in the west.

The U.K. has natural resources of oil and gas, which lie beneath the North Sea. Northern England, Scotland, and South Wales have traditionally been home to heavy industries such as mining and shipbuilding. These are gradually being replaced by newer ones such as the electronics, food-processing, and chemical industries. Many people work in service industries such as education, health care, and tourism. Much of the countryside in the U.K. is intensively farmed.

Many people in the Republic of Ireland also work in the service industries or in manufacturing industries. Farming is vital to the economy, with exports including butter, cheese and other dairy products, natural fibers, whisky, and beer.

England was conquered by the Romans and later by the Normans. It conquered Wales in the 1200s. England and Scotland have had the same monarch since 1603 and the same parliament since 1707. Ireland joined the union in 1801, but southern Ireland broke away in 1921.

BRONZE AGE
The Bronze Age followed the Stone Age. During this time, people used bronze instead of stone, flint, wood, and bone for their weapons and tools.

Bronze is a mixture of copper and tin. It can be hammered into many shapes to make weapons, tools, and jewelry. It was used by the

great early civilizations in the Middle East and Egypt. The Bronze Age lasted in Britain from 2500 B.C. until about 500 B.C.

BUDDHA AND BUDDHISM
Buddhism is one of the world's great religions. Its founder was Gautama, who lived from 563 B.C. to 483 B.C. He was rich, yet he was sad because he knew the world was full of suffering. So he gave up his riches, and spent many years trying to find the answer to the world's unhappiness.

Bronze Age: *Bronze Age metalworkers hammered complex patterns onto their pots.*

Buddha and Buddhism: *Buddha in a characteristic pose, with legs folded. His restful expression reflects a state of enlightenment and peace.*

He taught that there are eight "paths" to nirvana, or perfect peace. For this he was called Buddha, meaning "Enlightened One," and today millions of Buddhists around the world follow his teachings.

BUFFALO

Buffalo are wild cattle of Africa and Asia. There are several kinds.

The Indian water buffalo likes muddy swamps. It is a useful working animal, and gives meat and milk. The African or Cape buffalo cannot be tamed. It has massive horns and can be dangerous.

BULB

Plants make their own food, and some are able to store this food in special leaves, called bulbs.

An onion is a bulb. If you cut one open, you can see the closely packed layers of leaves. Daffodils, tulips, and hyacinths also have bulbs. In spring they use food from the bulb to make new leaves.

BUTTERFLY AND MOTH

Butterflies are among the most beautiful insects. They fly by day and their scaly wings are often brilliantly colored. Most moths are less colorful. Moths usually fly at dusk. Butterflies and moths belong to the same family. Moths have hairier bodies, and they fold their wings flat when resting, whereas butterflies hold their wings upright.

Female butterflies and moths lay eggs, which hatch into larvae, called caterpillars. Caterpillars eat almost nonstop and grow by shedding their skins. Some, like that of the cabbage butterfly, are harmful to crops. Others, like the silkworm, are useful.

When the caterpillar is full

Butterfly and Moth: *Butterflies are identified by their wonderfully patterned wings. In many species, the adults live only a few weeks.*

Painted lady (flying)

Painted lady (resting)

Small tortoiseshell (resting)

grown, it stops eating. It fastens itself to a leaf or a twig and becomes a chrysalis. Inside the hard case of the chrysalis the caterpillar changes its shape. When the chrysalis splits, the adult insect crawls out. As soon as its wings are dry, it flies away.

Small tortoiseshell (flying)

BYZANTINE EMPIRE

In A.D. 330 the Roman Emperor Constantine made the city of Byzantium the capital of the Roman Empire. He renamed it Constantinople. It later became the center of the rich and powerful Byzantine Empire.

This empire became the heart of Greek learning and Roman law because it was not plundered by barbarians, as Rome was after A.D. 476. The Greek Orthodox Church was also formed here.

The empire finally fell to the Turks in 1453.

Camberwell beauty (flying)

C

Caesar, Julius
(100–44 B.C.)

Julius Caesar was a Roman soldier, writer, and statesman. He was also a brilliant general. He conquered Gaul—what is today France, the Netherlands and Germany—and in 55, B.C. he successfully invaded Britain. He wrote a book about his military experiences.

He brought his army back to Italy in 49 B.C. After three years of civil war, he captured Rome and was declared dictator in 46 B.C. Caesar had many enemies. They thought he would make himself emperor, and assassinated him on the Ides (15th) of March, 44 B.C.

See also ROME, ANCIENT.

Calculator

Calculators are machines that help you solve mathematical problems. One of the first calculators was the abacus, which was used in the Middle East more than 5,000 years ago. Today most calculators are electronic and work very fast.

See also COMPUTER.

Calendar

A calendar is a way to divide to the year into months, weeks, and days. Almost everyone in the world uses the same kind of calendar. The Romans created our present calendar nearly 2,000 years ago. They based it on the movements of the Earth around the Sun, and the Moon around the Earth. In 1582, Pope Gregory XIII made some minor changes to the Roman calendar. This calendar, called the Gregorian calendar, is used today.

Camel

For thousands of years this strange-looking animal has been used to carry people and their goods. The camel is well adapted

Camel: The camel can withstand extremes of heat and cold, and can survive on salty vegetation.

36

Film wind-on lever

Series of mirrors directing light to the viewfinder

Viewfinder

Rewind crank

Film

Lens

Reflex mirror

Shutter

to desert life. It stores fat in its hump and can go for days without water. Its wide, padded feet do not sink into the sand.

The Bactrian camel from Asia has two humps. It can live in very cold regions. The Dromedary camel has only one hump.

CAMERA
A camera is a light box with a window, or lens, at the front. When you take a picture, a shutter moves aside and lets light from the object you are photographing pass to the back of the camera, where it hits a strip of

Camera: In a single-lens reflex camera, a mirror directs light entering the lens up to the viewfinder, allowing the image through the lens to be seen. When the shutter button is pressed, the mirror swings out of the way to allow light to reach the film.

light-sensitive film, forming an image of the object.

When the film is treated with certain chemicals, or developed, the image shows up. The developed film is called a negative. The process of printing changes the negative image into a positive picture on specially coated paper. The result is a photograph. It may be in black and white or in color, depending on the type of film used.

To take a clear photo, the correct amount of light must hit the film, and the lens must be focused on the subject. Some cameras make these adjustments automatically. Others have controls to allow you to do it more accurately yourself.

Cassettes and cartridges record moving images. Videocassettes carry reels of tape that record

Camouflage: Many insects mimic a feature of their surroundings, or another insect. Some look like leaves; stick insects look like twigs. Some flies look like stinging wasps, and some moths have an off-putting pattern on their wings.

both sound and pictures. A film cartridge is similar to a cassette but contains photographic film. The cartridge slots into a camera and, when exposed, is removed without any manual rewinding.

CAMOUFLAGE

Many animals are colored or shaped to match their environment. We call this camouflage. Camouflage makes an animal difficult to see, and so protects it from enemies.

Spots or stripes help to hide an animal by breaking up the outline of its body. The zebra's stripes blend with the long grass on which it grazes. The leopard's spots conceal it among the sun-dappled leaves of a tree.

Most fish have dark backs and light undersides. This makes them harder to see from above and

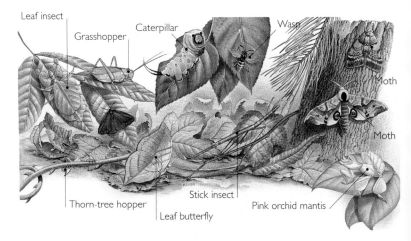

Leaf insect

Grasshopper

Caterpillar

Wasp

Moth

Moth

Thorn-tree hopper

Stick insect

Leaf butterfly

Pink orchid mantis

from below. Some animals trick their enemies by looking like something else. This is called mimicry.

Many insects and reptiles are so well camouflaged that it is hard to spot them until they move.

CANADA

Canada is a huge country. It covers the northern part of North America, stretching from the Atlantic Ocean in the east, to the Pacific in the west, and to the Arctic Ocean in the north. Altogether, it has an area of 3,850,000 sq. mi. Yet the population is very low—around 29 million people—and most of the country is empty.

Canada is a land of high mountains, thick forests, and vast plains. It has so many large lakes and rivers that more than 7 percent of its area is made up of fresh water.

Canada has a variety of climates. The west coast has cool summers and mild, wet winters. On the plains and in the east, the summers are hot and the winters cold. The north has short, cool summers and cold winters.

The land is very rich. The plains produce wheat and dairy products and timber comes from the forests. There are many minerals, such as coal, oil, natural gas, gold, and uranium. The rivers provide hydroelectricity.

Canada is divided into ten provinces and two territories. Each has its own government. The federal (central) government in the capital, Ottawa, makes laws for all of Canada.

See also PAGE 62.

CANAL

Canals are man-made rivers. Some are built to carry cargo boats, barges, and ships. Others provide water for irrigating the land. In some low-lying countries, canals drain the land. In Venice, Italy, canals form the "roads" of the city.

Some canals were built a very long time ago. Parts of the Grand Canal in China are more than 2,000 years old.

Today, the most important canals are the ship canals of Suez, Panama, and the St. Lawrence.

CANCER

Cancer is a dangerous disease that occurs through the uncontrolled growth of body cells. After heart disease, it is the leading cause of death in the world today.

Scientists everywhere are trying to find a cure for cancer. Many lives have been saved by educating people to spot cancer symptoms at an early stage, and through treatment by surgery, radiation, and drugs.

Car

Two German engineers, Karl Benz
and Gottlieb Daimler, built the
first cars in 1885 and 1886. These
had a gasoline engine, like most
modern cars. Later, some cars
were built with steam engines;
others were driven by electricity
from batteries. In the end, the
gasoline engine proved to be the
most successful.

At first, cars were handmade
and expensive. It was not until
1908 that they began to be made
cheaply. In that year Henry Ford
started to mass produce his Model
T, called the "Tin Lizzie." It
marked the beginning of the
modern car industry, which now
produces over 25 million cars a
year throughout the world.

A modern car is a collection of
10,000 or more separate parts.
These parts make up several basic
units: the body, the engine, and
the transmission are the main
units. The transmission carries
power from the engine to the
driving wheels. The other units
are the steering, the braking, and
the suspension.

See also FORD.

Carbon

Carbon is one of the chemical
elements. All living things contain
carbon. If you hold a plate above
a candle flame, a black deposit of
carbon forms on it. Both charcoal
and coke are forms of carbon. The
"lead" in pencils and diamonds are
natural forms of carbon.

Caribbean

The islands known as the West
Indies lie between the Caribbean
Sea and the Atlantic Ocean. The
many islands are divided into
more than 20 countries. The
largest are Cuba, Jamaica, Haiti,
and the Dominican Republic.

Most of the islands have a
tropical climate and people grow
sugar, tobacco, cocoa, coffee,
coconuts, bananas, and other
fruits. There is not much industry
but iron ore, bauxite, and asphalt
are mined. Many islands have a
busy tourist industry.

The West Indies were
discovered in 1492 by
Christopher Columbus. Spain
conquered the islands in the
1500s and later the British,
French, and Dutch set up colonies
there. African slaves were brought
to work on plantations. Today
most islands run their own affairs.
Most West Indians speak English,
French, or Spanish.

See also PAGES 62-63.

Castle

Hundreds of years ago a castle was
the safest place in times of war.
The earliest castles were wooden
forts. They were built on hilltops
and were surrounded by banks of

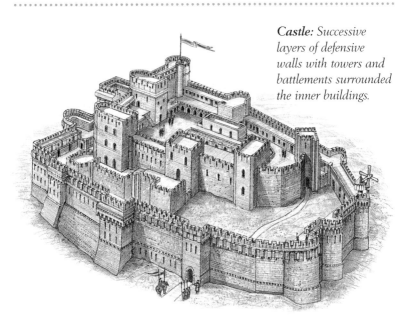

Castle: *Successive layers of defensive walls with towers and battlements surrounded the inner buildings.*

earth and ditches. Inside, there was room for the local people and their animals to take shelter.

In the Middle Ages castles were built from stone. The outer walls were high and thick. There were towers along the walls, with slits through which archers could fire arrows. Around the walls was a ditch, or moat, filled with water. In the center of the castle was a huge tower called a keep. Inside the keep, or in a separate building, was a great hall where the nobleman and his family lived, and a chapel. Elsewhere in the castle were kitchens, storerooms, barracks for soldiers, stables for animals, and a well.

It was difficult to capture a castle once the defenders had pulled up the drawbridge over the moat. Inside, they stored enough food and water to last for weeks. From the shelter of the castle walls they could shoot at the attackers, or drop boulders and boiling oil on top of them.

When an army attacked a castle, they surrounded the castle walls. If they failed to force their way in, they would try to starve the occupants out.

Although they must have been cold and damp, castles were good strongholds until cannons were invented. Cannonballs easily smashed stone walls.

CAT

A fluffy, playful kitten does not look very fierce. But it is a close relative of the mighty tiger. All cats are meat-eating mammals. They hunt by stealth, usually alone. They move soundlessly because their claws retract into soft pads on their feet. They can see well, even at night, and they have a keen sense of smell.

Domestic cats are descended from the African wildcat. The cat was sacred to the ancient Egyptians. In Europe, cats did not become common mouse-hunters until the 1700s.

There are many kinds, or species, of cats, and they make good pets. They are independent animals, however, and can go back to living in the wild very easily.

Abyssinian

Red point
Siamese

Cat: *Although there are many different breeds of cat, they do not vary very much from one another in overall shape and size. The main differences between breeds are largely those of coat length, color, and texture.*

Maine
coon

Cats can breed twice a year. The female usually gives birth to a litter of five or six kittens each time. The young of the big cats, such as lions and tigers, are called cubs. All cats, even well-fed pets, are hunters, and the big cats are the fiercest hunters of all

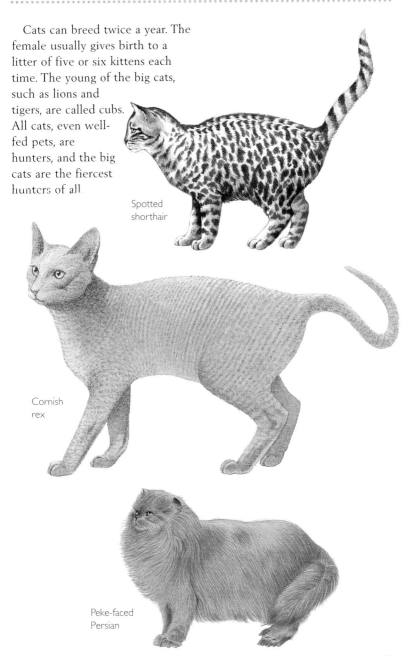

Spotted shorthair

Cornish rex

Peke-faced Persian

CATHEDRAL
See CHURCH.

CATTLE
Cattle is the term applied to animals such as buffalo, bison, and yaks, and bulls, oxen, and cows.

Cattle are kept to supply milk, meat, and hides. In many parts of Asia and Africa, they are also used to carry loads and pull carts.

People have kept cattle since ancient times. Pictures of them appear in Egyptian tomb drawings and reliefs.

CAVE
Caves are found in the sides of hills and cliffs. They are hollowed out of the rock by the sea or by underground streams.

Some caves were used by early people as places to live, and often contain relics and fossils.

See also STALACTITE AND STALAGMITE.

CELL
All living things are made up of cells. Most cells can only be seen under a microscope.

The animal called an amoeba has only one cell. The human body, on the other hand, has millions of cells, each with a job to do.

The center of a cell is the nucleus; around the nucleus is a blob of jelly called protoplasm.

Cave: Many cave systems occur in layered rock. People enter them via vertical cavities called potholes.

Pothole · Stalactite · Cave · Stream · Pool · Stalagmite

Cell wall

Protoplasm

Nucleus

Cell: The nucleus is surrounded by a gel-like substance where particles store and transform proteins and dispose of waste.

Cells join together to make tissues, —the materials from which our bodies are built. Different cells build skin, bone, blood, nerves, muscles, and glands. Cells reproduce by dividing. In this way, worn-out cells are replaced by new cells as we grow. Plants are also made up of cells.

CELTS

When we speak of Celts, we are really talking about people who speak Celtic languages.

The ancient Celts lived in northwestern Europe. They had loosely organized tribes made up of a chief, nobles, freemen, and slaves. They were very warlike and fought among themselves. They were good metalworkers, and gifted musicians and poets. Their religion was druidism. Celts may have arrived in Britain as early as 600 B.C. Later they were conquered by the Romans. Today the largest Celtic-speaking groups are found in Ireland, Scotland, and Wales.

CENTRAL AMERICA

Central America forms a bridge between North and South America. It consists of the independent republics of Costa

Celts: The Celts were skilled craftsmen, and their work often used animal forms.

45

Rica, El Salvador, Guatemala, Honduras, Panama, Nicaragua, and Belize. It was created millions of years ago by volcanic activity and its landscape ranges from desert to rain forests, swamps, and beaches.

Most people in Central America are *mestizos*, a mixture of Spanish and Indian. Spanish is the main language, but English and various native languages are also spoken. Tropical crops, such as sugar, bananas, cotton, and coffee, are the main produce.

CEREALS

Cereals are important food crops. They belong to the grass family. The fruit or seed of the plant is

Cereals: The different types of cereals are all high in nourishment.

called a grain. In tropical lands the most important cereals are rice, maize, and millet. In cooler climates the main cereals are wheat, oats, barley, and rye.

Rice is the main food for over half the people in the world. It grows in warm and wet climates and needs plenty of water.

Much of the world's wheat is grown on the plains of Canada, the United States, Australia, and Russia. The grain is ground into flour and used to make bread, pasta, and breakfast foods.

CHARLEMAGNE (A.D. 742–814)

The name Charlemagne means "Charles the Great." He was king of a people called the Franks and he conquered and ruled a huge empire in Europe. This Christian

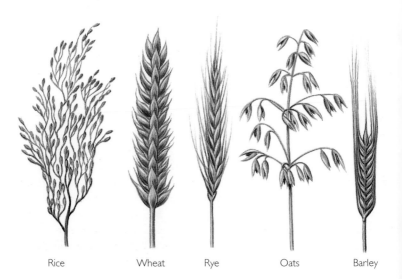

Rice   Wheat   Rye   Oats   Barley

empire was the greatest since the time of Rome, and became known as the Holy Roman Empire.

Charlemagne and his warriors fought against many enemies, including the Moors in Spain. As well as being a great soldier, Charlemagne also built schools and libraries. Scholars from all over Europe came to his court.

CHAUCER, GEOFFREY (*c.*1342–1400)

Chaucer was a great English poet whose most famous work is *The Canterbury Tales*. He was the first important author to write in English rather than Latin.

The Canterbury Tales is a collection of stories told by an imaginary group of people on a pilgrimage to the tomb of St. Thomas à Becket in Canterbury.

CHEESE

Cheese is made from the solid part, or curd, of sour milk. Bacteria are added to milk to make it sour, and the curd is separated from the watery part, or whey. The curd is then heated, pressed, and allowed to cool.

There are many different kinds of cheese. Cheddar, Cheshire, and Stilton cheeses come from England. Cheeses such as Roquefort (France) and Gorgonzola (Italy) have blue veins in them. These are caused by special molds.

CHEMISTRY

Chemistry is one of the main branches of science. The people who practice chemistry are called chemists. They look into the properties and makeup of matter. They try to find out what substances are made of, how they are put together, and how they react with other substances.

CHESS

This is a game that has been played for hundreds of years. It probably came from India, where it was known in the 7th century, and had reached Europe by the 11th century.

Chess is played by two players on a board with 64 squares. Each player has 16 pieces, and the pieces move in different ways. They attack and defend, and can be captured and removed from play. The king is the most important piece and the game is won when one player takes the other's king.

CHINA

China is the world's third-largest country. About one-fifth of the world's people are Chinese. For much of its history, China was cut off from the rest of the world.

China became a united empire more than 2,000 years ago. The land was ruled by royal families called dynasties. To keep out nomadic enemies, the emperor Shih Huang Ti built the Great Wall of China. Writing, music, and painting flourished. Wise men studied the works of such teachers as Confucius and Lao Tse.

Cities and roads were built, and merchants sailed as far as Africa and India. The Chinese invented paper and printing, and discovered how to make silk and gunpowder. Their fine pottery, or porcelain, was so famous that we still call all crockery "china."

For centuries the Chinese did not want anything to do with the outside world. But gradually China was made weak by civil wars and bad government. Europeans started trading in China in the 1800s and tried to run things for their own advantage. China even had to give pieces of land to them. For example, it gave the island of Hong Kong to the British in 1842.

At first the Chinese were unable to stop the Europeans. Then, in the early 1900s, they overthrew the last of the emperors and set up a republic. Later, China was split by fighting between communists and nationalists. Before World War II Japan invaded China. By 1949, the communists had won the civil war and China, led by Mao Tse-tung, became a communist state. By the late 1900s, China was

becoming powerful once more. In 1997, it took back Hong Kong from the British.

See also PAGE 62.

CHRISTIANITY

Christianity is one of the world's great religions. Christians follow the teachings of Jesus Christ, whom they believe is the son of God who came to live on earth in human form.

There are more than one billion people on earth who call themselves Christians. They belong to many different sects, or groups. But all accept the Bible as their holy book. The most important Christian festivals are Christmas, which celebrates Christ's birth, and Easter, which marks his death and resurrection. Christian worship takes place on Sunday, a holy day and day of rest.

Christianity is almost 2,000 years old. We date our calendar from the year in which it is thought Jesus was born.

See also JESUS CHRIST.

CHURCH

Christians began to build churches when the Roman emperor Constantine was converted in the 4th century and they no longer had to worship in secret. These early buildings were patterned after the Roman basilica—an oblong hall with aisles and an spires, tall, narrow arches, stained-glass windows, and lots of stone carvings. Such churches were to inspire awe and wonder in the worshiper.

The most splendid churches are often cathedrals. A cathedral is the most important church in an area called a diocese, headed by a bishop. The cathedral contains the bishop's *cathedra* (seat), or throne. Many magnificent cathedrals were built in Europe in the Middle Ages. Most have beautiful carvings, statues, and stained-glass windows. Built to glorify God, they demanded the best engineering skills of their time.

Church: *Florence Cathedral was started in 1296, and is mainly Gothic in style. Its huge dome was built in the 1400s.*

apse, or rounded part, at the end. Later, a transept, or two wings were often added to make the shape of a cross.

From the 5th to the 12th centuries, many churches adopted the Romanesque style, which had round arches and thick walls. In the Middle Ages the Gothic style appeared. This featured pointed

CHURCHILL,
WINSTON
(1874–1965)

Churchill was prime minister of Britain during World War II.

One of Churchill's ancestors was a great English general, the Duke of Marlborough (1650–1722). Churchill led an adventurous life as a soldier and newspaper reporter before he became a politician. But his greatest years were from 1940 to 1945, when his stirring speeches and strong leadership encouraged people during the war against Hitler's Germany.

CIVIL RIGHTS MOVEMENT
See KING, MARTIN LUTHER.

CIVIL WAR
A war fought between citizens of the same country is called a civil war. Sometimes a civil war produces a great change in a country's history.

The American Civil War (1861–1865) was fought between the government (Union), backed by the northern states, and the (Confederacy) southern states. The war was fought over the rights of each state to make its own laws, in particular the laws regarding slavery. In 1860, the southern states thought that the new Republican president, Abraham Lincoln, would abolish slavery. The large farms, or plantations, of the South depended on slave labor, and the owners thought that the abolition of slavery would ruin them.

In 1861, the 11 southern states decided to break away, or secede, and form a separate nation, the Confederate States of America. War broke out in April, when the Confederates fired on Fort Sumter in Charleston harbor, South Carolina. At first the war went well for the South. Under their brilliant commander, Robert E. Lee, the South won a victory at the Battle of Bull Run in July 1861. But in 1863 the tide turned after the Battle of Gettysburg, in

Union flag

Union soldier

Confederate flag

Confederate soldier

Civil War: *In the American Civil War, the Union (the northern states) and the Confederacy (the southern states) each had their own uniform and flag.*

Pennsylvania. In 1864, General Ulysses S. Grant took command of the Union armies, and in April 1865 Lee surrendered. Both sides had suffered tremendous losses.

In England, the last civil war was fought from 1642 to 1649. It was a battle for power between the king, Charles I, and Parliament. Charles thought that he had a divine, or God-given, right to rule the country. Parliament thought he was too extravagant. Charles finally dismissed Parliament in 1642 and called his supporters to arms. They were called Royalists.

The parliamentary soldiers were the Roundheads. Led by Oliver Cromwell, they defeated the Royalists and captured the king. Charles was put on trial and executed in 1649. England became a monarchy once more in 1660, but the king never again had as much power as before the Civil War.

In the late 1900s, there have been many civil wars in Africa, Latin America, and Southeast Asia.

CIVILIZATION

Civilization began when people no longer had to spend all their time searching for food. Farming and trade developed as people settled in one area. As they grew more prosperous, they built cities, temples, and roads. They

developed languages, and expressed themselves through art, music, and theater. Most civilizations in ancient times had strong armies and spread their way of life by conquest.

Only the ruins of these great civilizations of the past now remain. But they have left their mark on our lives. Civilization in Europe today, for example, owes a great deal to the ideas of the Greeks and Romans. The modern world is a mixture of civilizations.

CLEOPATRA (69–30 B.C.)

Cleopatra, Queen of Egypt, was one of the most beautiful and fascinating women in history. Two famous Roman rulers, Julius Caesar and Mark Antony, fell in love with her. Antony even gave parts of the Roman Empire to Cleopatra. The angry Romans declared war on Antony, and defeated him. Both Antony and Cleopatra killed themselves.

CLIMATE

Climate means the typical weather of a place over a long period of time.

Several factors affect climate. One is latitude—a place's distance from the equator. The Sun's rays are most direct at the equator, so it is hotter there. At the poles, the rays spread over a large land area and it is cool. A second factor is

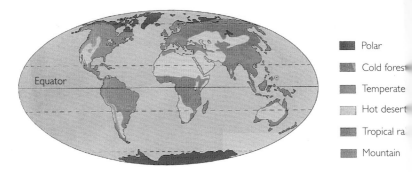

Polar

Cold forest

Temperate

Hot desert

Tropical ra

Mountain

Equator

Climate: The world is divided into climate zones. Places all around the world that are in the same zone have a similar kind of climate.

how close a place is to the sea. Water heats and cools more slowly than land. Away from the sea, land becomes much hotter in the summer and colder in winter.

The main elements of climate are temperature and rainfall. The world's climatic regions are based on average temperatures and rainfall figures over many years.

CLOCK AND WATCH

A clock is an instrument for measuring the time. A watch works in a similar way and is small enough to carry around.

Although the Chinese probably had clocks as early as A.D. 600, the earliest European clocks were made around 1200. They were made by blacksmiths and were often basic and awkward. They worked by the force of gravity

(weights) and were not accurate. A more accurate clock was developed when Galileo discovered that a pendulum could be used to regulate time. Since then, clocks have been continuously improved and ordinary clocks are accurate to within a few minutes a year.

Today, two very precise clocks are used. One is the quartz crystal clock. The second is the cesium atomic clock, which keeps time to within a second in a million years.

See also GALILEO.

CLOUD

After it has rained, the puddles soon dry. The water has turned into invisible water vapor.

Water vapor rises into the air, and the higher it rises, the cooler it becomes. As it cools, the vapor turns back into water. Millions of tiny drops of water, so light they float in the air, make clouds.

When the air can hold the water droplets no longer, they fall as rain. When the air is very cold, they

---

turn to ice and fall as hail or snow.

By studying the different kinds of cloud, scientists can tell what sort of weather to expect.

See also FOG; RAIN, RAIN AND HAIL; WATER.

COAL

Coal is one of our most important fuels. It can be burned to heat buildings. At power plants it is burned to make electricity. Coal is also made into coal gas and coke,

Cloud: *Cumulus, stratocumulus, altocumulus, and cirrus are fair-weather clouds; altostratus, cirrostratus, nimbostratus, and cumulonimbus are rain-bearing.*

which are both good fuels. A lot of coke is used in the steel industry. Many chemicals can be produced from coal to make dyes, plastics, medicines, and explosives.

Coal is mined from the ground. It is formed from the remains of forests of huge ferns and strange trees that grew millions of years ago. When these died, they were covered by mud and sand. In time, the mud and sand changed into rocks. The dead plants were squeezed until they changed into coal. Most coal is deep underground and mining it is expensive and dangerous.

See also MINING.

Cocoa

Cocoa comes from the seeds of the cacao tree, which is grown in West Africa, the West Indies, and South America. Chocolate is made from cocoa and was first introduced, as a drink, to Europe from the New World by the Spanish in the 1500s.

Coffee

Coffee is made from the roasted and ground beans of the coffee plant. Coffee bushes grow best in warm, wet highland areas, such as in Brazil and Kenya. Inside each red berry are one or two beans. At harvesttime, the beans are removed and dried in the sun. Then they are roasted until they are brown, and sold, either ground or whole.

Color

White light is actually a mixture of all colors. It is only when white light is split up, as it is in a rainbow, that we see its range of different colors.

The first person to understand light and color was Sir Isaac Newton. In 1666, by passing light through a glass prism (a triangular solid block of glass), he obtained all the colors of a rainbow. This band of color is called the spectrum. Newton then combined the colors again by passing them

Cocoa: A South American woman harvests cocoa. The beans are dried, roasted, and ground into a thick brown liquid, which, when dried, makes cocoa powder.

Color: When light beams in the three primary colors are mixed, they make white light. But when the same colors are mixed in the form of paint, they make black.

through a second prism to form white light. The colors of the spectrum are always in the same order—red, orange, yellow, green, blue, indigo, and violet.

We see the color of an object, such as a yellow flower, because all the other colors are absorbed and only the yellow is reflected. A white flower reflects all the colors of light.

COLUMBUS, CHRISTOPHER (1451–1506)

This Italian explorer discovered America by accident. He believed he could reach the Indies (Asia) by sailing west, instead of east, for he was sure the Earth was round. He persuaded the King of Spain to let him try, and in 1492 he set out with three ships, *Santa Maria*, *Pinta*, and *Nina*, across the Atlantic Ocean. When he reached the Caribbean islands, Columbus thought he had reached Asia, so he called them the "Indies."

Comet: A comet sends out a trail of dust and gas, which can be seen as a tail streaming away from it.

COMET

Comets are heavenly bodies. They are glowing balls of gas and dust that travel in an orbit, or path, around the Sun. Some of them have long tails, but they only start to glow when they get near the Sun. Some comets take only a few years to circle the Sun, others take thousands of years. The most famous comet is Halley's Comet, which orbits the Sun every 76 years or so.

COMMONWEALTH

Most of the countries that were part of the British Empire now belong to the Commonwealth of Nations. It includes huge countries, such as Australia, Canada, and India, and many tiny islands. Nearly all the members are self-governing, but their laws, schools, and way of life are often similar. Some still trade mainly with Britain. The richer members try to help the poorer countries, and Commonwealth leaders meet regularly to discuss their economic and financial problems.

COMMUNICATION

The exchange of information, ideas, or feelings is called communication. Animals communicate with one another, but human beings have the most complicated forms of communication.

Speech was the earliest means of human communication. The Sumerians were the first to invent writing, and the Phoenicians developed the first alphabet sometime before 1000 B.C.

Until the 1400s, all books in Europe were handwritten. Then Johannes Gutenberg invented a system of printing from movable type. Communication took a giant step forward, with the printing of many copies of books, newspapers, and eventually magazines.

The invention of photography brought about visual communication through pictures and films, and electricity made communication over huge distances possible, by way of the telegraph, telephone, radio, and television. Computers have revolutionized modern communications because they can store, sort, and provide information at amazing speed.

COMMUNISM

The main idea behind communism is that wealth should be shared. So communist governments control all factories, mines, farms, and stores.

Karl Marx and Friedrich Engels put forward communist ideals in the 1800s. The first country to have a communist government was the U.S.S.R., after the 1917 revolution. Later, much of eastern Europe and Cuba also became communist, along with China.

The situation changed quickly after 1990, when the U.S.S.R. and other eastern European countries abandoned communism.

COMPASS

A compass is an instrument used to find directions. A simple compass has a needle that always points in the same direction— north and south. This is a magnetic compass, and it works the way it does because the Earth itself acts like a big magnet. The compass needle lines up parallel with the Earth's magnetic field.

Most ships and planes use a gyrocompass. This device contains a spinning drum and, once set, its axis always points in one direction, no matter which way the ship or plane turns.

COMPUTER

Computers are electronic machines, like calculators. But computers do more than figure out mathematical problems. They can process information. This means that they can be given information, store it, and sort through it in order to carry out a task. They can also work at incredible speeds.

Computers cannot think. They have to have instructions, called programs, to tell them what to do with the information they are given. These programs can be changed so that computers can do an enormous number of different things. Today, computers are found in offices, hospitals, factories, schools, and homes. They can send spacecraft to outer planets, help to forecast the weather, run machines, and play exciting games.

Every computer has four main parts. The input is where the computer receives instructions and information; the central processing unit (C.P.U.) is where calculations are carried out; the memory is

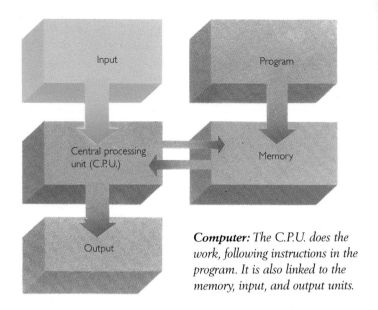

Computer: *The C.P.U. does the work, following instructions in the program. It is also linked to the memory, input, and output units.*

where information and instructions are stored; and the output is where the result is displayed or printed out.

The first computer, E.N.I.A.C., was built in 1946. It filled a whole room. Today the programs to run a computer can be held electronically on tiny silicon chips. The largest computers are called mainframes. They can service several hundred users. The smallest are called laptops. The Internet is a vast network that allows people with computers to communicate anywhere in the world.

See also CALCULATOR; ELECTRONICS; INTERNET; SILICON CHIP.

CONFUCIUS (*c.*551–479 B.C.) China's most famous thinker and teacher was born into poverty. Confucius disliked the misery and disorder he saw all around him and wanted to do something about it. He did this by gathering together groups of followers and teaching them how to lead good lives. He taught them that all people should try to love and understand others. People should become rulers because they were good, not just because they were strong or came from powerful families. His followers helped to spread his teachings long after he died at the age of about 70.

CONIFER

Conifers are plants that have cones instead of flowers for making pollen and seeds. They are all trees or shrubs, and are mainly found in the cool parts of the world. Conifers include cedars, larches, pines, firs, and spruces. Most of them have thin, needle-like leaves that they do not shed in winter.

CONSERVATION

Conservation is the protection of nature, including natural resources such as water, soil, minerals, forests, and wildlife.

For centuries, people have made use of these resources without any thought of preserving them. Conservationists try to prevent the pollution of our earth, air, and water, and the destruction and disappearance of rare animals and their habitats.

CONSTELLATION

From earliest times people have studied the night sky. It did not take them long to realize that the sky had a systematic pattern of stars in fixed groups, or constellations. People saw the shapes of animals and the heroes of their myths, and named groups of stars after them.

Some constellations always come up in the east in a certain order just before sunrise and seem to travel in the same path as the Sun. These are the 12 figures or signs of the zodiac.

There are 88 constellations. The Greeks identified and named 48 of them. Some constellations can be seen only in the Northern Hemisphere and some only in the Southern Hemisphere.

See also ASTRONOMY; STAR; UNIVERSE.

COOK, CAPTAIN JAMES (1728–1779)

James Cook made three voyages of discovery to the Pacific and Antarctic oceans. The first was an expedition to the South Seas in 1768. He sailed to Tahiti and then to New Zealand. In 1770 he reached Botany Bay in Australia and claimed it for Britain.

On his second voyage (1772–1775), he sailed more than 60,000 miles, going right around the world. On his third expedition he discovered the Hawaiian Islands. He was killed there by the inhabitants.

See also EXPLORERS.

COPERNICUS, NICOLAUS (1473–1543)

Copernicus was a Polish astronomer. He showed that the Earth was not the center of the universe. He stated that the Earth revolves once every 24 hours, that it travels around the Sun once a year, and that it and the other planets form the solar system.

See also ASTRONOMY.

COPPER

Copper was one of the first metals to be used. To begin with, people used pure copper, which they found in the ground. Later, people learned how to extract it from ore by smelting.

Pure copper is very soft. It is often mixed with other metals to make a harder alloy such as brass.

See also ALLOY; METALS.

CORTÉS, HERNAN (1485–1547)

Cortés was a Spanish soldier who conquered the Aztec Empire in Mexico between 1519 and 1521 with fewer than 600 men.

Cortés: Cortés governed Mexico for nine years.

Cortés had guns, which gave him great power over the people, and they thought he was a god.

COTTON

Cotton is a very useful plant. Inside its round fruit, called bolls, are lots of white fibers. When the fruit ripens, it splits open and the fibers are blown away, spreading the seeds. On cotton plantations the bolls are picked before this can happen, and the fibers are processed into the different types of cotton fabrics.

Cotton grows best in warm, wet lands, including Asia, the southern United States, India, China, Egypt, and Brazil.

COUNTRIES OF THE WORLD

There are more than 180 independent countries in the world, and they exist in all shapes and sizes. The following list shows the situation at the end of 1997.

EUROPE

Country	Population	Capital
Albania	3,441,000	Tirana
Andorra	62,500	Andorra-la-Vella
Austria	7,968,000	Vienna
Belarus	10,141,000	Minsk
Belgium	10,113,000	Brussels
Bosnia-Herzegovina	3,459,000	Sarajevo
Bulgaria	10,319,000	Sofia
Croatia	4,495,000	Zagreb
Czech Republic	10,296,000	Prague
Denmark	5,215,718	Copenhagen
Estonia	1,530,000	Tallinn
Finland	5,107,000	Helsinki
France	57,981,000	Paris
Georgia	5,457,000	Tbilisi
Germany	81,591,000	Berlin
Gibraltar	29,000	Gibraltar
Greece	10,451,000	Athens
Hungary	10,115,000	Budapest
Iceland	269,000	Reykjavík
Ireland	3,553,000	Dublin
Italy	57,023,000	Rome

Country	Population	Capital
Latvia	2,557,000	Riga
Liechtenstein	30,629	Vaduz
Lithuania	3,700,000	Vilnius
Luxembourg	401,000	Luxembourg
Macedonia*	2,571,000	Skopje
Malta	370,402	Valletta
Moldova	4,432,000	Kishinev
Monaco	31,000	Monaco-Ville
Netherlands	15,503,000	Amsterdam; The Hague (seat of govt.)
Norway	4,337,000	Oslo
Poland	38,388,000	Warsaw
Portugal	9,823,000	Lisbon
Romania	22,835,000	Bucharest
Russia	147,000,000	Moscow
San Marino	25,000	San Marino
Slovakia	5,353,000	Bratislava
Slovenia	1,946,000	Ljubljana
Spain	39,621,000	Madrid
Sweden	8,780,000	Stockholm
Switzerland	7,202,000	Bern
Ukraine	51,380,000	Kiev
United Kingdom	58,258,000	London
Vatican City	1,000	Vatican City
Yugoslavia* (Serbia-Montenegro)	10,849,200	Belgrade

AFRICA

Country	Population	Capital
Algeria	27,939,000	Algiers
Angola	11,072,000	Luanda
Benin	5,409,000	Porto Novo
Botswana	1,487,000	Gaborone
Burkina Faso	8,769,000	Ouagadougou
Burundi	6,393,000	Bujumbura
Cameroon	13,233,000	Yaoundé
Cape Verde Is.	359,500	Praia
Central African Republic	3,315,000	Bangui
Chad	6,361,000	N'djaména
Comoros	544,000	Moroni
Congo	2,590,000	Brazzaville
Côte d'Ivoire	14,253,000	Yamoussoukro
Democratic Rep. of Congo	43,901,000	Kinshasa
Djibouti	586,000	Djibouti
Egypt	62,931,000	Cairo
Equatorial Guinea	400,000	Malabo
Eritrea	3,531,000	Asmara
Ethiopia	55,053,000	Addis Ababa
Gabon	1,320,000	Libreville
Gambia	1,118,000	Banjul
Ghana	17,453,000	Accra
Guinea	6,700,000	Conakry
Guinea-Bissau	1,073,000	Bissau
Kenya	28,261,000	Nairobi
Lesotho	2,050,000	Maseru
Liberia	3,039,000	Monrovia
Libya	5,407,000	Tripoli
Madagascar	14,763,000	Antananarivo
Malawi	11,129,000	Lilongwe
Mali	10,759,000	Bamako
Mauritania	2,274,000	Nouakchott
Mauritius	1,117,000	Port Louis
Morocco	27,028,000	Rabat
Mozambique	16,004,000	Maputo
Namibia	1,540,000	Windhoek
Niger	9,151,000	Niamey
Nigeria	111,721,000	Abuja
Rwanda	7,952,000	Kigali
São Tomé & Príncipe	131,100	São Tomé
Senegal	8,312,000	Dakar
Seychelles	73,000	Victoria
Sierra Leone	4,509,000	Freetown
Somalia	9,250,000	Mogadishu
South Africa	41,465,000	Pretoria (administration); Cape Town (legislature); Bloemfontein (judiciary)
Sudan	28,098,000	Khartoum
Swaziland	855,000	Mbabane
Tanzania	29,685,000	Dodoma
Togo	4,138,000	Lomé
Tunisia	8,896,000	Tunis
Uganda	21,297,000	Kampala
Zambia	9,456,000	Lusaka
Zimbabwe	11,261,000	Harare

*Not internationally recognized

ASIA

Country	Population	Capital
Afghanistan	20,141,000	Kabul
Armenia	3,599,000	Yerevan
Azerbaijan	7,558,000	Baku
Bahrain	568,000	Manama
Bangladesh	120,433,000	Dhaka
Bhutan	1,638,000	Thimbhu
Brunei	284,500	Bandar Seri Begawan
Cambodia	10,251,000	Phnom Penh
China	1,221,462,000	Beijing (Peking)
Cyprus	729,800	Nicosia
Hong Kong	6,189,800	Victoria
India	935,744,000	Delhi
Indonesia	197,588,000	Jakarta
Iran	67,283,000	Tehran
Iraq	20,449,000	Baghdad
Israel	5,629,000	Jerusalem
Japan	125,095,000	Tokyo
Jordan	5,439,000	Amman
Kazakhstan	17,111,000	Alma-Ata
Korea (N)	23,917,000	Pyongyang
Korea (S)	44,995,000	Seoul
Kuwait	1,547,000	Kuwait
Kyrgyzstan	4,745,000	Bishkek
Laos	4,882,000	Vientiane
Lebanon	3,009,000	Beirut
Macao	395,300	Macao
Malaysia	20,140,000	Kuala Lumpur
Maldives	238,000	Malé
Mongolia	2,410,000	Ulan Bator
Myanmar	46,527,000	Rangoon
Nepal	21,918,000	Katmandu
Oman	2,163,000	Muscat
Pakistan	140,497,000	Islamabad
Philippines	67,581,000	Manila
Qatar	359,000	Doha
Saudi Arabia	17,880,000	Riyadh
Singapore	2,848,000	Singapore
Sri Lanka	18,354,000	Colombo
Syria	14,661,000	Damascus
Taiwan	21,200,000	Taipei
Tajikistan	6,101,000	Dushanbe
Thailand	58,791,000	Bangkok
Turkey	61,945,000	Ankara
Turkmenistan	4,099,000	Ashkhabad
United Arab Emirates	1,904,000	Abu Dhabi
Uzbekistan	22,843,000	Tashkent
Vietnam	74,545,000	Hanoi
Yemen	14,501,000	San'a

SOUTH AMERICA

Country	Population	Capital
Argentina	34,587,000	Buenos Aires
Bolivia	7,414,000	La Paz (seat of government); Sucre (legal capital)
Brazil	161,790,000	Brasilía
Chile	14,262,000	Santiago
Colombia	35,101,000	Bogotá
Ecuador	11,460,000	Quito
French Guiana	98,000	Cayenne
Guyana	835,000	Georgetown
Paraguay	4,960,000	Asunción
Peru	23,780,000	Lima
Suriname	412,000	Paramaribo
Uruguay	3,168,000	Montevideo
Venezuela	21,844,000	Caracas

NORTH AND CENTRAL AMERICA, AND THE WEST INDIES

Country	Population	Capital
Anguilla (Br.)	8,960	The Valley
Antigua and Barbuda	64,166	St. John's
Bahamas	275,700	Nassau
Barbados	264,300	Bridgetown
Belize	215,000	Belmopan
Bermuda	72,000	Hamilton
Canada	29,463,000	Ottawa
Costa Rica	3,424,000	San José
Cuba	11,041,000	Havana
Dominica	74,200	Roseau
Dominican Republic	7,823,000	Santo Domingo

El Salvador	5,768,000	San Salvador
Greenland (Dan.)	55,000	Godthaab
Grenada	96,000	St. George's
Guadeloupe (Fr.)	387,000	Basse-Terre
Guatemala	10,621,000	Guatemala City
Haiti	7,180,000	Port-au-Prince
Honduras	5,654,000	Tegucigalpa
Jamaica	2,447,000	Kingston
Martinique (Fr.)	359,600	Fort-de-France
Mexico	93,674,000	Mexico City
Nicaragua	4,433,000	Managua
Panama	2,631,000	Panama City
Puerto Rico (U.S.)	3,300,000	San Juan
St. Kitts-Nevis	41,000	Basseterre
St. Lucia	141,000	Castries
St. Vincent and the Grenadines	111,000	Kingstown
Trinidad and Tobago	1,306,000	Port-of-Spain
United States of America	263,250,000	Washington, D.C.

AUSTRALASIA

Country	Population	Capital
Australia	18,088,000	Canberra
Fiji	784,000	Suva
Kiribati	80,000	Baraiki
Marshall Islands	54,000	Majuro
Micronesia	121,000	Kolonia
Nauru	11,000	Nauru
New Caledonia	171,000	Nouméa
New Zealand	3,575,000	Wellington
Niue	2,500	Alofi
Palau	17,000	Koror
Papua New Guinea	4,302,000	Port Moresby
Solomon Islands	378,000	Honiara
Tonga	98,000	Nuku'alofa
Tuvalu	9,000	Fongafale
Vanuatu	165,000	Port Vila
Samoa	169,000	Apia

CRAB

Along with shrimp, prawn, and lobsters, crabs belong to the group of animals called crustaceans.

Most crabs live in the sea. They have jointed legs, like insects, and walk sideways. They seize food in their strong pincers, or claws.

There are around 5,000 different kinds of crabs. They vary in size from tiny pea crabs less than 1/2 inch across to giant crabs measuring 1 foot or more.

Crab: The edible crab can be 5 inches long.

CRICKET

The game of cricket began in the 1700s. It is played by two teams of 11 players, using a wooden bat and a leather ball. Each team takes it in turn to "bat" and to "field." The batsmen try to score "runs" by hitting the ball when it is bowled to them. The bowler, helped by fielders, tries to get the batsmen "out."

CROCODILE AND ALLIGATOR

These reptiles are related. They both have tough, armored skin and their ears, eyes, and nostrils are located at the top of their heads. Unlike most reptiles, crocodiles and alligators lay their eggs in a nest or heap of dead leaves and plants. As the plants rot, they provide heat, which helps to hatch the eggs.

Crocodiles live in Africa, Asia, and Australia. They eat fish, birds, turtles, and water mammals. They vary in size from 5 feet to 20 feet and have narrow, pointed heads.

Alligators live in the United States and China, where they can grow as big as crocodiles. They mainly eat fish.

Crocodile and Alligator:
Crocodiles use their long, pointed teeth to spear fish and to grasp the flesh of animals they prey on.

CROMWELL, OLIVER (1599–1658)

Cromwell was one of the most famous men in English history. He helped to lead Parliament's army to victory over the Royalists in the Civil War, and became Lord Protector from 1653 to 1658. He also signed the warrant for the execution of Charles I.

See also CIVIL WAR.

CRUSADES

The Crusades were wars in which Christian armies fought to win back the Holy Land of Palestine from the Muslims.

The First Crusade began in 1096 after Pope Urban II had called on the Christians of Europe to capture Jerusalem, which was a sacred city to the Muslims as well as the Christians. Many knights answered the call, and the First Crusade was a great success. The crusaders captured Jerusalem in 1099. The Muslims were not beaten, however. In 1187, led by the great sultan Saladin, they recaptured Jerusalem.

There were eight Crusades in all, and thousands of crusaders went to the Holy Land. Before the Muslims finally defeated them in 1303, many crusaders had died of sickness or in battle.

The Crusades brought Europeans into contact with the way of life of the East.

They learned Eastern medicine and science, and were encouraged to trade for the riches of the East.

CURIE, MARIE (1867–1934) AND PIERRE (1859–1906)

The Curies, who were husband and wife, were among the earliest scientists to study radioactivity, the powerful rays given off by some rare materials.

In 1898 the Curies discovered and worked on the radioactive elements, polonium and radium. They shared a Nobel prize in physics in 1903 with Henri Becquerel for their work. Madame Curie was awarded a second Nobel prize, in chemistry, in 1911 for her further work on radium.

See also RADIOACTIVITY.

CUSTER, GEORGE (1839–1876)

George Armstrong Custer was an army officer who died at the Battle of Little Bighorn (also known as "Custer's Last Stand"). He became the youngest general in the Union army during the Civil War. Custer later commanded the Seventh Cavalry in many brutal attacks on the Sioux and Cheyenne tribes before the famous battle in which he and all his men were killed.

CYCLONE

See HURRICANE AND TORNADO.

D

DAM

A dam is a barrier built across a river or lake. Some dams are built to create a reservoir for storing water, others to control flooding or to produce water power for making electricity.

Some dams are made from earth or rock fill, others are made from concrete. There are two main types of concrete dam: gravity dams resist the horizontal thrust of the water through the weight of the dam itself; arch dams curve upstream in the center, enabling them to resist the force of the water. At 1,100 feet high from its foundations, the Rogun dam in Tajikistan is the world's highest dam.

DANCE

People have danced to music since the beginnings of history, and many different countries and regions of the world still have their own special traditions of "folk" dance—for example, Scottish reels and Irish jigs.

In modern times, dance crazes have often swept across the Western world. One of the first was the craze in the early 1800s for dancing the waltz, which started in Germany. In the early 1900s, there were crazes for the tango, which started in South America, and many other dances. Today the most popular kind of social dancing is probably freestyle dancing to recorded pop music.

In folk dances, people usually dance in small groups. For dances like the waltz and tango, people usually dance in pairs, and in disco dancing they sometimes dance without a partner at all.

Dance can also be performed by trained dancers on a stage. An example of this is ballet. Classical ballet is based on a number of set positions and movements that are arranged by a choreographer in different combinations and sequences to tell a story or to act out an idea or feeling. Ballet was first recognized in France, where the Royal Academy of Dancing was founded in 1661. Modern ballet allows dancers more freedom of movement and expression.

Ballet steps are recorded on paper using special symbols, so that the same ballet can be danced by different ballet companies at different times. Some of the ballets performed today were first presented 140 years ago.

DARWIN, CHARLES ROBERT (1809–1882)

Darwin was a great naturalist whose theory of evolution sought to explain why there are so many different kinds of plants and animals. Darwin said that those animals and plants whose slight differences made them able to live in their environment more easily would survive and pass on their differences to their offspring.

Darwin presented this idea of natural selection in his book, *On the Origin of Species,* in 1859.

DEER

Deer are hoofed mammals that run swiftly to escape their enemies. Like antelope and cattle, deer chew the cud. Usually only the stags (males) have horns, or antlers. Females are called hinds.

Deer live in cooler climates than antelope. Most deer live in woodland, feeding on grass and leaves. The reindeer, or caribou, lives on the cold northern tundra. The largest deer is the moose of North America.

DEMOCRACY

The word democracy comes from two Greek words and means "government by the people." In ancient times emperors and kings had great power to make laws and collect taxes. In a democracy a group of men and women elected by the people make the laws.

Some democracies are republics, in which the head of state is a president elected by the people. Others have a king or queen,

although the country is governed by parliament. If the people living in a democracy do not like their government, they vote against it at an election.

DESERT

Not all deserts are hot and sandy. Some are cold and rocky. All get very little rain and snow. About one-fifth of the Earth's land surface is desert.

Most deserts are in the middle of continents. There is little rain,

Deer: The stag sheds his antlers each year and grows a new, larger pair. He uses them for fighting other stags.

Desert: Cacti survive in the desert because they store water in their fleshy stems.

because the moist winds from the sea are dry by the time they reach these areas. As there are no clouds, a desert may get very hot during the day. At night, the ground loses heat and the desert becomes cold.

Desert: An oasis occurs in the desert where there is an underground supply of water.

Strong winds blow away the soil, leaving bare rock, or sweep the sand into great waves called dunes. It is difficult for plants to live in such conditions. Many desert animals shelter from the sun during the day and come out at night. Some never drink, but get moisture from their food.

The world's largest desert is the Sahara in Africa. There are other huge deserts in central Asia (the Gobi), in southern Africa, Australia, India, and in North and South America.

DICKENS, CHARLES JOHN HUFFAM (1812–1870)
Dickens is one of the greatest English novelists. He created many famous characters, like

Scrooge in *A Christmas Carol*, and often wrote about children. In *David Copperfield* he described his own boyhood. Though his books contain humorous characters, they also tell of the poverty, crime, and cruelty of his day. Dickens's writing encouraged people to do something about these problems.

DIGESTION

The food we eat must be broken down inside the body before it can be absorbed by the blood and used for nourishment and energy. This happens in the digestive system.

Digestion begins in the mouth, where food is chewed into small pieces and mixed with saliva, before being pushed down into the stomach. The stomach churns the food, mixing it with gastric juices, and turns it into a soft paste, which passes slowly into the small intestine.

Inside the small intestine, food is mixed with bile from the liver and juice from the pancreas, which break it down more. Much of this fluid passes through the wall of the small intestine into the blood. The waste passes into the

Digestion: *A meal takes between 10 and 20 hours to travel through the different parts of the human digestive system.*

large intestine and leaves the body as feces.

DINOSAUR

See PREHISTORIC ANIMALS.

DISEASE

When something goes wrong with a part of your body, you may be suffering from a disease.

Many diseases are infectious. They are caused by attacks on the body by tiny living things. Bacteria cause diseases such as typhoid and tuberculosis. Viruses give us influenza, measles, and the common cold.

Diseases can also be caused by poor diet and a lack of vitamins. Sometimes glands can go wrong and upset the way the body works. Other diseases are hereditary, and can be passed on from parents to children.

Drugs can cure many diseases, and vaccination protects us from others.

See also BACTERIA; DRUGS; MEDICINE; VITAMIN.

DIVING, SCUBA

To stay underwater for more than a few minutes, divers must wear breathing equipment. In shallow waters divers use air tanks. These supply them with compressed air through a mouthpiece. Deep-sea divers wear a special pressure suit pumped up with air.

DNA AND RNA

See GENETICS.

DOG

The dog was the first animal to be tamed by human beings. Cavemen probably reared wild dog pups and trained them to hunt.

Today, there are many different kinds, or breeds, of dogs. Each breed has qualities that suit it to particular tasks. Spaniels and retrievers are good at retrieving

Field spaniel

Shih tzu

Pug

game. German shepherds and Dobermans make excellent guard dogs. Hounds follow a scent. Sheepdogs control a flock of sheep. And many breeds make excellent companions.

Even though the dog has lived close to people for so long, it still has the instincts of a wild animal. Before going to sleep, a dog will turn around and around—as if making a bed in dry leaves. Because wild dogs live in packs, or groups, the dog's instinct is to follow and obey the pack leader. This makes it easy to train, as its master becomes the "pack leader."

The wild members of the dog family include coyotes, foxes, jackals, and wolves.

Doberman

French bulldog

Boston terrier

Greyhound

Dog: Dogs come in a huge range of shapes and sizes, depending on the purpose for which they were originally bred.

71

DOLPHIN

Dolphins are small whales. They live in the sea or in big rivers, and they eat fish. Dolphins are mammals, so they have to come to the surface to breathe. They are marvelous swimmers and often play by leaping right out of the water and twisting around.

DRAGON

A dragon is a fabulous, invented monster. It is often represented as a gigantic reptile with a lion's claws, the tail of a serpent, wings and scaly skin, and breathing fire.

Mainly we think of dragons as being evil, fearful creatures, but this is not so in all cultures. The Chinese believe that the sign of the dragon can protect them from evil or injury.

DRUGS

Herbs and chemicals that are used to cure diseases are called drugs. Some mosses and herbs contain healing substances that have been known to people since the earliest times. By the 1600s, nearly every town had an apothecary, or pharmacist, who made up pills and mixtures. Many of these did nothing at all.

In the 1800s, the first man-made drugs, produced from chemicals, were used to treat disease. A great step forward was the discovery of penicillin in 1928. This was the first antibiotic drug, the type that kills harmful bacteria.

Drugs can be dangerous if they are not used properly. People can become addicted to certain drugs and cannot live without them.

See also DISEASE.

DYE

Dyes are substances used to color fabrics and other materials. Some dyes come from plants and animals. A red dye called madder comes from the roots of the madder plant. Cochineal is a scarlet dye obtained from the cochineal insect. Most dyes used today are made from chemicals. Many of these man-made dyes have brilliant colors.

DYNAMITE

In 1866 Alfred Nobel, a Swedish chemist, accidentally made an important discovery. He mixed a very dangerous explosive called nitroglycerin with a kind of sandy earth called *kieselg-uhr*. The mixture turned into a solid cheeselike substance that could be handled safely but was still a powerful explosive. He called it dynamite.

Nobel made a fortune from explosives. With some of the money he set up a fund to give yearly prizes to scientists and writers whose work has helped mankind. These are known as Nobel prizes.

E

Outer ear

Eardrum

Malleus

Cochlea

Incus

Stapes

EAGLE
These birds
of prey are the
kings of the bird
world. Eagles can fly
to great heights. The
largest eagles, such as
the golden eagle, can
carry off lambs and
even young deer in their
strong claws.

Today, eagles are protected by
law. Eagles are becoming rare
because people have shot and
poisoned so many of them.

EAR
Any sound causes vibrations,
which are passed by the outer
ear down to the eardrum. The
eardrum then vibrates, just like the
skin of a musical drum. Three tiny
bones in the middle ear pick up
and pass on the vibrations. Inside
the inner ear is a shell-like tube
full of fluid called the cochlea.

*Ear: The three bones of the middle
ear are the malleus, the incus, and
the stapes. They magnify sounds
about 20 times.*

The vibrating air makes the fluid
vibrate, too. Nerves send messages
about the vibrations to the brain.
And when the brain has figured
out what the messages mean, we
"hear" the sounds.

The inner ear also helps us keep
our balance by means of fluid-
filled tubes.

*Eagle: Some eagles are
huge, with wingspans of
more than 6 feet.*

EARTH

The Earth we live on is one of nine planets that orbit the Sun. Scientists think the Earth was probably formed from a spinning cloud of gas and dust. From the age of the oldest rocks we know that the Earth is more than four billion years old.

The Earth has an invisible outer covering called the atmosphere. The atmosphere lies in several layers. The outer edge is about 1,000 miles from the Earth. The lowest layer, the troposphere, is where life exists.

The Earth is the only planet with large amounts of surface water. Oceans and seas cover 70 percent of its surface. The water was formed by chemical reactions after the Earth had become a solid ball of rock.

The Earth is rocky, and very rugged in places. It is made of igneous, or crystallized, rocks and sedimentary, or deposited, rocks. The surface is called the crust.

Earth: The Earth gets hotter toward its center. Temperatures in the inner core are probably around 9000°F.

Crust

Mantle

Outer core

Inner co

Epicenter

Hypocenter

Shock waves spread outward

Below the crust is the mantle. This is a thick layer of heavier rocks, up to 1,800 miles deep. Below this the rocks are molten (melted) because it is so hot. At the center of the Earth is a core of solid rock, probably made of nickel and iron. The core acts as a giant magnet.

See also CALENDAR; FOSSIL; MOUNTAIN; OCEAN; RIVER; ROCK; SOLAR SYSTEM; VOLCANO.

EARTHQUAKE

The Earth's crust is made of plates of rock that can move and crack. When they shift like this, the ground shakes, causing an earthquake.

Not all earthquakes are major, destructive movements. Around 20 severe earthquakes occur

Earthquake: The hypocenter is where the rock plates shift suddenly. The epicenter is the point above it on the Earth's surface.

each year. But there are about a million minor tremors as well. Earthquakes are detected by instruments called seismometers.

When an earthquake occurs on the ocean floor it produces great waves called tsunamis. They travel long distances at speeds of up to 500 mph. In the open ocean they may be only 3 feet or so high, but when they run into shallow water and slow down they rise rapidly to heights of 30 feet to 100 feet.

See also VOLCANO.

EARTHWORM

See WORM.

EASTERN EUROPE AND THE BALKANS

The countries of eastern Europe include Poland, Hungary, the Czech Republic, Slovakia, Romania, Bulgaria, Albania, the former states of Yugoslavia, and the western states of the former Soviet Union—Ukraine, Moldova, and Belarus. Much of the region is mountainous and much of it has large forests and fertile plains. Agriculture plays an important role in all economies and many of the countries have large industries. The region has natural resources such as timber, oil, coal, natural gas, and iron ore.

For much of the late 1900s, all of the countries were under communist rule. The first democratic elections did not take place until the late 1980s and 1990s. While some countries re-established themselves peacefully, there have been devastating wars in others, such as the former states of Yugoslavia.

ECHO

Sometimes when we shout, the sound of our voice comes back again a few seconds later. This is an echo. It happens when the sound is reflected by an object some distance away. Bats use sound echoes to find the insects that they eat. Ships and submarines use sound echoes (sonar) to detect objects underwater. Airports use echoes of radio waves (radar) to track aircraft.

ECLIPSE

When one heavenly body passes in front of another and blots out its light, we say that an eclipse is taking place. The Moon can cause an eclipse of the Sun. This happens when the Moon passes in front of the Sun and blots out the Sun's light. The Moon's shadow falls on the Earth and the sky goes dark. Then, as the Moon's shadow passes by, daylight returns. An eclipse of the Moon occurs when it moves into the shadow of the Earth.

Eclipse: In a solar eclipse the Moon comes between the Sun and the Earth.

Edison: Thomas Edison invented the phonograph in 1877. It was the ancestor of the record player and all modern sound systems.

ECOLOGY

Ecology is the study of plants and animals and how they live in their natural communities. This science shows how living things make use of their surroundings, or environment, and how they affect one another.

Most plants and animals can live only in a particular kind of environment such as a desert, a pond, a marsh, or a forest. Each plant is suited to the temperature, soil, and water supply of the ground in which it grows. Animals eat the plants or other animals. This link between plants and animals is called a food chain.

EDISON, THOMAS A. (1847–1931)

Edison was one of the world's greatest inventors. He patented nearly 1,300 inventions. Among these were the phonograph, the electric light, and an electric generating station. He said that he owed his success not to genius but to hard work.

EEL

The life story of the common eel is very strange. These eels live in rivers in Europe and North America, but they migrate to the sea to breed. They make an amazing journey, swimming downstream and even wriggling overland until they reach the sea. The eels lay their eggs far out in the Atlantic Ocean, and then they die. The young eels, called elvers, swim back to the rivers. The long journey can take three years.

Some eels, such as the conger eel, spend all their lives in the sea.

EGG

All animal life comes from some kind of egg. Some are laid by the female and develop outside her body before they hatch. Most mammals develop inside the mother's body. The egg, or ovum, must be joined with a sperm cell from the male in order to develop.

EGYPT

Modern Egypt is a country of more than 62 million people. Nearly all of them live in only

Egg: The different fluids inside a bird's egg provide the embryo with the nutrients it needs.

4 percent of the country's total area (387,000 sq. mi.). This is the land irrigated by the Nile. The rest is desert.

Most Egyptians work on the land. They produce cotton, rice, fruits, grain, and vegetables. In some areas modern irrigation has been so successful that two or three crops are grown in a year.

Egypt is an independent Arab republic. The major religion is Islam and the language is Arabic.

See also PAGE 61.

EGYPT, ANCIENT

The civilization of ancient Egypt was centered on the Nile River. The Nile Valley is hot and dry, but each year the river floods and spreads a rich silt over the land, making it fertile. The ancient Egyptians worshiped the Nile as a god.

The pharaohs (kings) of Egypt were very powerful. The people thought the pharaoh was a god. He owned everything and everyone had to obey his commands. The pharaohs built huge tombs, often in the form of pyramids. The dead pharaoh was buried inside, surrounded by treasure and by all the things that he would need in the next world, such as food, clothes, furniture, and weapons. The dead body was

Egypt, Ancient: Important people's bodies were preserved using special chemicals. The preserved bodies are called mummies.

preserved, or mummified, before being buried.

Rich Egyptians enjoyed lives of luxury. They had servants, slaves, dancers, and musicians. Ancient Egyptian civilization began around 3200 B.C. and lasted until 30 B.C., when Egypt was finally conquered by the Romans.

EINSTEIN, ALBERT (1879–1955)

Einstein was one of the most brilliant thinkers of modern times. He completely changed our ideas about space, time, and motion, and about matter and energy. Einstein said that nothing can travel faster than light, and that mass and energy are different forms of the same thing. His ideas were shown in his famous laws of relativity.

ELECTRICITY

Electricity is a form of energy. The electricity we use in our homes is produced by generators in power plants. A battery is a portable supply of electricity.

Electricity flows through wires as electric current. It is a flow of electrons, tiny particles present in all atoms. They flow easily in metals, which are called good conductors of electricity.

Electricity: In a simple electrical generator, a coil of wire is turned between the poles of a magnet, generating an electrical current.

Current can only flow if a wire makes a complete loop or circuit. Switches operate gaps in the circuit to start or stop the flow of electricity.

ELECTRONICS

Electronics is the study of the way electrons act as they flow through certain crystals, gases, or a vacuum. Electrons are tiny particles found in all atoms. Electronic devices like transistors and silicon chips are used in radios, televisions, and computers.

See also COMPUTER; RADAR; RADIO; SILICON CHIP; TELEVISION; TRANSISTOR.

ELEMENT AND COMPOUND

Elements are the building blocks from which all substances are formed. When a chemist splits up salt, he finds that it is made of two substances called sodium and chlorine. No matter how hard he tries, he cannot split sodium and chlorine any further. They are chemical elements.

In nature there are 92 elements, and scientists have made another 17.

Elements are made of atoms. Groups of atoms joined together are called molecules. For example, a molecule of oxygen consists of two oxygen atoms. A substance whose molecules contain more than one kind of atom is called a compound. Most elements are found as chemical compounds.

ELEPHANT

The elephant is the largest living land animal. A big male, or bull, may weigh 7 tons. Elephants

Electronics: A silicon chip.

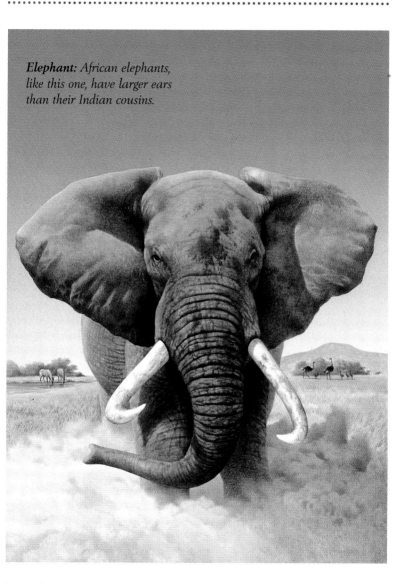

Elephant: African elephants, like this one, have larger ears than their Indian cousins.

live in herds. If one elephant is injured, the rest will help it. Elephants eat huge amounts of grass and tree leaves every day.

There are two kinds of elephant. The Indian one can be trained to work. The larger African elephant is not easily tamed.

81

ELIZABETH I (1533–1603)

When Elizabeth was born, her father, Henry VIII, was furious. He wanted a son to succeed him as King of England. But when Elizabeth became queen in 1558, she proved a strong ruler. She never married, and for 45 years successfully protected England against its chief enemies, France and Spain. Daring sailors, such as Francis Drake, and brilliant writers, like William Shakespeare, made her reign one of the most exciting in English history.

ENERGY

When a piece of wood is set on fire, it burns and gives out light you can see and heat you can feel. Heat and light are two common forms of energy.

Wood is one kind of fuel that releases energy when burned. Coal, gasoline, and natural gas are other fuels. When gasoline is burned in a car engine, the energy produced makes pistons turn the car wheels.

The chemical energy in the fuel is turned into mechanical energy to turn the car wheels. When the car is moving, it has kinetic energy—the energy of motion. A rock balancing on top of a cliff has potential energy—the energy of position.

Energy: Wind generators harness wind power to make electricity—but they are expensive.

ENGINE

We use many kinds of engine in the modern world to work the machines in our homes and factories, and the ones that transport us in the air and on sea and land. Most engines burn fuel to produce energy. A car engine burns gasoline, while trucks and buses have diesel engines, which burn oil. Aircraft have jet engines, which burn kerosene (paraffin). There are all kinds of internal combustion engines, in which fuel is burned in an enclosed space. Steam engines and turbines burn fuel outside of the engine.

See also ENERGY; FUEL; JET ENGINE.

EROSION

Erosion happens when parts of the Earth's surface are worn away or shaped by water, wind, or ice. The sea beating against a coast, for example, often wears it away or erodes it. After rain, water pours down a mountainside and may erode the soil covering it. Winds, too, may erode soil, whipping it into the air and carrying it away. The ice in glaciers grinds away at rock, eroding it. Erosion is a problem for farmers, because it carries away the soil in which they plant their crops. Mountain farmers often build steplike terraces down mountain slopes to keep this from happening.

EUROPE

The continent of Europe is smaller than any of the other continents except Australia, yet a fifth of the world's people live in Europe.

Most of Europe has fertile soil and good rainfall. Europe's farmers produce meat, grain, fruit, and vegetables. Most farms use modern machinery. Europe is rich in coal, iron ore, and other raw materials.

Europe lives on trade. It has good highways, railroads, airports, and canals. Ships carry goods across the Baltic Sea, the North Sea, and the Mediterranean Sea, and to all parts of the world.

The people of Europe come from many different nations. Each has its own language and customs. In the past, European countries fought with each other. European wars affected the rest of the world, because European countries were so powerful. Two world wars in the 1900s started in Europe.

For many years after World War II there was hostility between communist eastern Europe and the democratic West. But that ended with the sudden decline of communism in the late 1980s and early 1990s. In recent years, most of Europe has worked together to bring peace to the region.

EUROPEAN UNION

The E.U., or European Union (which used to be known as the European Community or Common Market), is a group of countries mainly in western Europe. In 1997, there were 15 members: Austria, Belgium, Denmark, Finland, France, Germany, Greece, Ireland, Italy, Luxembourg, the Netherlands, Portugal, Spain, Sweden, and the United Kingdom. These countries all work and trade together. The E.U. has a civil service and a parliament. There is also a European Court of Justice.

EVOLUTION

Evolution is the gradual process by which all living things have changed since life began millions of years ago. Fossils show us how creatures have changed.

The first creatures were very simple forms of life. They evolved into more complicated plants and animals. Fish evolved from smaller sea creatures. Some fish began breathing air and crawled onto dry land. These were the first amphibians. The amphibians evolved into reptiles. All birds and mammals, including humans, evolved from reptiles.

EXPLORERS

People have always had the urge to explore the unknown.

Some explorers have gone in search of lands to settle. Others wanted riches, while some explorers journeyed only in search of knowledge.

To the ancient peoples of Europe, "the world" meant the lands around the Mediterranean Sea. Only the Phoenicians dared to sail out into the gray Atlantic Ocean beyond.

In the 900s, the Vikings sailed in their small, fragile ships as far as North America. But until the invention of the magnetic compass in the 1300s, long sea voyages were very dangerous.

To reach the East, with its gold, spices, and silks, European merchants had to travel overland. Marco Polo reached China in 1275. Then the Portuguese discovered that they could reach India by sailing around the coast of Africa. In 1492, Columbus reached America, the "New World." By 1522, Magellan's sailors had proved that the world was round by sailing around it.

After this, explorers left Europe eager to find lands to settle as colonies. The last continent to be explored by Europeans was Africa. During the 1800s, several explorers crossed this unknown continent.

In 1909, Peary reached the North Pole, and in 1911 Amundsen beat Scott to the South Pole. Today few

Explorers: *Columbus and the other explorers of his time sailed the world's oceans in small but sturdy ships called caravels.*

parts of the Earth are unexplored.

See also COLUMBUS; COOK; GAMA; MAGELLAN; MARCO POLO; VIKING.

EYE

Our eyes are very delicate. Each eye is a ball full of liquid. In the center of the front is a black hole called the pupil. This lets in light. Behind the pupil is a lens. The lens focuses an image of whatever we are looking at onto a screen called the retina. Then messages are sent along a nerve to the brain. The brain arranges the messages into a picture again, and we "see."

The colored part of the eye is called the iris. It is a ring of muscle that makes the pupil larger or smaller. In bright light, the pupil gets smaller. But in dim light, it gets larger to let in as much light as possible.

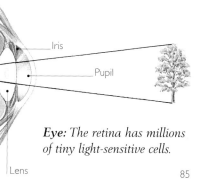

Retina

Iris

Pupil

Optic nerve

Lens

Eye: *The retina has millions of tiny light-sensitive cells.*

85

F

Farming

Farming is the world's most important industry. By raising animals and growing crops, farmers provide us with the food we eat. Civilization became possible only when people stopped being nomadic and settled down to farm.

Gradually, people learned how to plant seeds and grow crops, and how to keep and breed animals such as chickens, cattle, and sheep. Slowly, tools were devised to help.

In the 1800s and 1900s, machines were invented to do the work of people and animals. There were better ploughs, seed drills, threshers, and reapers, and tractors replaced the horse and ox. Discoveries about crop rotation, fertilizers, and chemicals allowed farmers to grow larger crops.

Fertilizers are important because they add vital plant food to the soil. Plants grown for their crops need some substances, such as nitrogen, phosphorus, and potassium, in greater amounts than are usually found in the soil. Fertilizers replenish the levels of these substances. Some are made from natural substances; others are mainly chemicals.

Fern

Ferns are primitive plants. There have been ferns on the Earth for more than 300 million years. Many prehistoric ferns were as tall as trees; a few tree ferns still grow in tropical forests.

Ferns have no flowers or seeds. Instead they have tiny cells called spores under their leaves. The wind scatters the spores onto the ground and they eventually grow into new ferns.

Fiber Optics

An optical fiber is a glass or plastic strand along which light, including laser light, can be sent on a curved path. Each fiber can be as little as $1/2000$ inch to

Fiber Optics: Optical fibers have many uses. Doctors use them to see inside the body.

$1/200$ inch thick. The fibers are mostly used in bundles. Fiber optics are now used instead of metal wires for telephone systems, because a single fiber can carry thousands of telephone conversations at the same time.

See also LASER.

FILM

"Moving pictures" were first shown in the 1890s. People crowded into movie theaters to watch them. During the 1930s, because of its good weather and varied scenery, Hollywood became the center of the movie industry. At first movies were silent and somewhat jerky. "Talking pictures" appeared in 1927.

The person who decides how a story is made into a movie is the director. The producer takes care of the business side. And, in addition to the actors and cameramen, there are people to do the scenery, lighting, costumes, makeup, and "stunts." Sometimes a studio set, with artificial scenery, is used. But movies are often "shot" (filmed) outside "on location." When filming is over, the best parts of the movie are edited (cut up and run together) to make the finished movie.

FINGERPRINT

The tiny ridges and furrows arranged in patterns on the tips of the fingers and thumbs are called fingerprints. No two people have the same fingerprints. Even if the outer skin is damaged, the pattern does not change. This is the reason why fingerprints are

Fingerprint: Police experts classify fingerprints by their basic patterns and by the numbers of ridges.

Arch   Whorl

Loop   Composite

so helpful to the police in identifying criminals.

FISH

Fish are animals that spend their lives in water. Some fish live in saltwater and some live in freshwater. Some spend part of their lives in the sea, and part in the rivers.

Most fish have bony skeletons. But a small group, including sharks,

Fish: These North American freshwater fish have also been introduced into parts of Europe.

Rock bass

Pumpkinseed

have skeletons made of cartilage. Like all animals, fish have to breathe oxygen. Their gills take oxygen from the water. Some fish breathe through their skins as well, and a few have lungs.

Fish eat water animals, including other fish, and plants. They swim by bending their bodies from side to side, and by moving their tails. They use their fins to keep them upright and for steering and braking.

Most fish are covered with scales. Some fish have a line of special scales along each side of the body. This is called the lateral line. It helps the fish detect underwater vibrations. Most fish have an air bladder inside their bodies to keep them at any level they choose. But the more primitive cartilage fish do not have this "swim bladder." If they stop swimming, they sink.

During the breeding season, some fish migrate long distances to reach their spawning grounds. Most fish lay their eggs and leave them floating in the water. Out of millions of eggs, only a few survive. Other fish lay fewer eggs, but take more care of them.

See also EEL; SEA HORSE; SHARK.

FISHING

Most fish are caught in the sea, but in some countries river and lake fisheries are important. The best fishing grounds are in the Atlantic and Pacific oceans.

The most important food fish are cod, mackerel, haddock, herring, flatfish (such as flounder and sole), sardines, tuna, and salmon. Shellfish, such as shrimp, lobsters, and oysters, also make valuable catches.

Most sea fish are caught in nets. Trawls are long, bag-shaped nets towed along underwater. A purse-seine net is drawn around a shoal of fish, then pulled up. Gill nets look like draperies: the fish swim into them and are caught in the meshes. Fish can also be caught on baited lines. This method is known as trolling.

FLAG

Every country has its own flag. Organizations such as the United Nations and the Red Cross have flags, and kings and queens have their own personal flags.

Fishing: Most fish are caught using trawls. Seines are good with fish such as herrings, which gather in shoals near the surface.

The first flags were ornamental streamers. In battle, flags or standards, raised high on poles, were rallying points for soldiers.

In the Middle Ages there were several flags of different shapes, (gonfalons, banners, and pennons) but today most are rectangular. Flags are also used at sea to identify ships and to send messages.

FLOWER

Most plants have flowers. The flower is the part of the plant where the seeds develop. Without it, the plant could not reproduce itself. Inside each seed is all the "information" needed to make a new plant grow. Most flowers appear in the summer when the

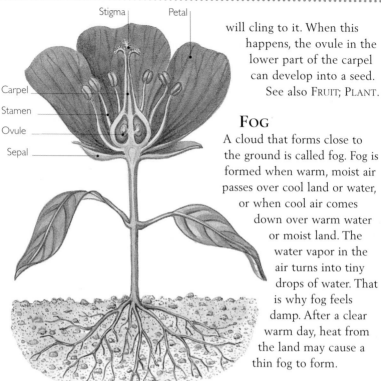

Stigma | Petal

Carpel

Stamen

Ovule

Sepal

Flower: A flower's colorful petals attract birds and insects, which then help to spread the powdery pollen onto the sticky stigma.

plant is full-grown. Flowers come in all shapes and sizes, but they all have the same basic parts.

The most important parts are called stamens and carpels. The stamens are male parts, which produce a powder called pollen. The carpels are female parts. Each carpel has a sticky top, called a stigma. It is sticky so that pollen

will cling to it. When this happens, the ovule in the lower part of the carpel can develop into a seed. See also FRUIT; PLANT.

FOG

A cloud that forms close to the ground is called fog. Fog is formed when warm, moist air passes over cool land or water, or when cool air comes down over warm water or moist land. The water vapor in the air turns into tiny drops of water. That is why fog feels damp. After a clear warm day, heat from the land may cause a thin fog to form.

FOOD

Our bodies need energy to live and grow. This energy comes from the food we eat. The three most important substances in food are carbohydrates, fats, and proteins. Carbohydrates are food "fuels." They give us energy to work, move, and keep warm. Sugar and starch are carbohydrates. We eat carbohydrates in bread, potatoes, rice, candy, and cakes. Cream, butter, and the fat in meat provide us with fats. These are also good fuels. If we eat too many carbohydrates or fats, our bodies store what they cannot use. Then we get fat. Proteins build the body's cells and are vital to good health. Eggs, lean meat, cheese, fish, and legumes are rich in proteins.

FOOTBALL

Football is a very popular sport in the United States. Each team has 11 players, all wearing protective equipment. The teams try to get the ball past their opponents' goal to score points. The game involves kicking, passing, carrying the ball, and tackling, and each team member has a different job to do.

Football is played by elementary school, high school, college, and professional teams. The professionals play in the National Football League (NFL). The NFL consists of 28 teams, and is divided into two conferences, the American Football Conference and the National Football Conference. Each has three divisions: Eastern, Central, and Western. The teams in each division represent different U.S. cities.

There are 16 scheduled games in the NFL regular season, which lead to the play-offs. The play-offs determine the two conference champions. These two teams then play

the NFL title in the Super Bowl.

Football was developed during the mid-1800s. It came from soccer and rugby, which were both developed in England. Soccer is called football in most countries, but it is very different from American football. For example, in soccer, handling the ball is not allowed. Soccer is played in more places and by more people than any other kind of football. In recent years, it has become increasingly popular in the United States.

FORD, HENRY (1863–1947)

Henry Ford was an American automobile manufacturer. He was the first man to develop assembly-line methods of production. In mass production the parts of the car are added to the car body on a conveyor. Ford could produce many cars

Ford: Model T.

Forest: Countries such as New Zealand have mixed forests, with both conifers and broad-leaved trees.

very cheaply. Between 1908 and 1927 he mass-produced 15 million Model T cars.

FOREST

Land that is covered with trees is forest. Today about a third of the Earth's land surface is covered by forests. There are about 20,000 different kinds of tree, and around 1,000 of them produce good timber.

In cold lands, the forests are mainly of conifers, such as pines and firs. The largest coniferous forests are in northern Europe, Canada, and Siberia.

Milder countries have forests of broad-leaved trees, such as oaks, elms, beeches, birches, and maples. These trees are deciduous, they shed their leaves every year.

In the hot, wet lands close to the equator there are tropical forests of trees such as ebony and mahogany, whose wood is very hard. There are vast rain forests in South America, central Africa, and Southeast Asia. Swamp forests of mangroves are often found near coasts.

FOSSIL

Fossils are the hardened remains of dead animals and plants that lived thousands of years ago. They tell us what life was like before written records were kept.

Some fossils are the impressions

Fossil: By studying fossils, experts can discover much about the far-distant history of the Earth and the creatures that have inhabited it.

turned into rock. Sometimes a whole body is preserved, including the hair and skin. Sometimes the body has dissolved away and the space it left filled with mud or sand that slowly turned into rock. Most commonly, though, fossils are the remains of the hard parts of animals such as bones or shells.

made by remains that have since disappeared. They are often found in rock because the plants and animals were covered by mud or sand, which later

Fox: Foxes can adapt to most environments, including cities.

FOX

Foxes belong to the dog family. They hunt at night for rabbits, mice, and voles. The female fox is called a vixen. She rears her cubs in an underground den.

Farmers dislike foxes, because they kill other animals. In Britain and some other countries the fox is hunted by foxhounds. Silver and blue arctic foxes are bred on special farms for their fur. The little fennec fox lives in the desert.

FRANCE

France is the largest country in western Europe. Its beautiful scenery includes forests, plains, valleys, high mountains, and great rivers.

France has fertile soil and a mild climate. Many of its people are farmers. France is famous for its wine and cheese. France has many industries and is a member of the E.U. Its capital city is Paris.

In 1789, the French people overthrew their king and set up a republic. This important event is called the French Revolution.

See also PAGE 60.

FREUD, SIGMUND (1856–1939)

Sigmund Freud was an Austrian doctor who made a great contribution to the study of the human mind. He taught that the subconscious, the activity of the mind that we are not aware of, provides clues to a person's mental state. He also developed psychoanalysis, a kind of examination of the mind.

FROG AND TOAD

These animals are amphibians. They can live on land, but must return to the water to lay eggs.

Frogs and toads look similar. But frogs use their long back

Frog and Toad: Tree frogs have suction pads on their toes that help them cling to branches.

Fruit: Many fruits are sweet and juicy, so that animals will carry them away as food and help to spread the seed.

Plum

Pear

Orange

legs to hop, whereas toads crawl or run. Both eat insects and worms, catching their prey with their long, sticky tongues.

In spring frogs and toads travel to ponds and streams to breed. They lay eggs called spawn. The eggs hatch into tadpoles. Tadpoles swim like fish and breathe through gills. But soon they grow legs, lose their tails, and develop lungs. Finally, they become tiny frogs or toads.

FRUIT

We all recognize apples, oranges, plums, and pears as fruit. But pea pods, walnuts, tomatoes, acorns, and cucumbers are also fruit. Many kinds of fruit are good to eat. Growing fruit is an important industry.

The fruit is the part of a plant that protects the seed. It helps to spread the seed so that new plants can grow. Some fruit has wings (such as the sycamore) or light, fluffy heads (such as the dandelion) so that the seeds will blow away. Burrs are a kind of fruit that clings to the fur of passing animals. Many kinds of fruit split when ripe, letting their seeds fall. Some fruit, like the coconut, is dispersed by floating on water.

See also FLOWER; PLANT.

FUEL

Fuels are substances that release energy when burned. The process of burning is called combustion.

Fuel may be solid, liquid, or gas. Coal, wood, charcoal, and peat are solid fuels. The most important liquid fuels come from petroleum. Natural gas, a compound of hydrogen and carbon, is often found near petroleum.

G

GALAXY

Our Sun is part of a great family of stars called the Milky Way galaxy. A galaxy is a big group of stars held together by gravity.

A galaxy like ours contains about 100 billion stars and probably many planets. Some stars are grouped together in giant clusters. The galaxies also contain great clouds of gas and dust called nebulae.

GALILEO (1564–1642)

Galileo was an Italian astronomer. In 1609, he became the first person to look at the sky through a telescope. He saw the mountains on our Moon and the moons of the planet Jupiter.

Galaxy: The Milky Way, our galaxy, is a huge spiral. We are part of the solar system, which lies toward the edge of the galaxy.

Galileo was skilled at mathematics and carried out scientific experiments. He discovered how a pendulum swings and showed that different weights fall to the ground at the same rate.

GAMA, VASCO DA (*c.*1469–1524)

This Portuguese explorer was the first man to find a sea route to India. He sailed from Lisbon in July 1497, rounded the Cape of Good Hope in November, and went on to land in southwestern India in May 1498. He returned to Portugal with two ships loaded with spices.

GANDHI, MOHANDAS KARAMCHAND (1869–1948)

Gandhi helped to free India from British rule. Known as the Mahatma or "Great Soul," he believed that all violence was wrong. So he used "peaceful noncooperation" as a weapon.

He was born in India. From 1893 to 1915, he worked in South

Africa. When India became independent in 1947, Muslims and Hindus began fighting. Gandhi failed to make peace between them, and was shot by a Hindu fanatic on January 30, 1948.

GARIBALDI,
GIUSEPPE (1807–1882)
Garibaldi was an Italian patriot. In his time Italy was made up of several separate states, and large parts of northern Italy belonged to Austria. Garibaldi fought to make Italy one country from 1834 until 1860. Then Victor Emmanuel became king of the whole of Italy.

GEM
Some rocks contain crystals that can be cut to show great brilliance and sparkle. They are called gems or gemstones. They can be set in gold or silver to form jewelry.

The finest gems are diamonds. They are a form of carbon. Diamonds are expensive because they are rare, and difficult to cut.

Gem: Around one hundred different kinds of gemstones are found in the Earth's rocks.

They are the hardest of all the minerals. Some diamonds are made into cutting tools.

Some gems are not crystals, but beautiful stones. They include opal and lapis lazuli. Pearls are gems that oysters produce in their shells.

GENETICS
The science of genetics explains why living things look and behave as they do. Advanced animals have two sexes, male and female. Each individual produces sex cells. If a

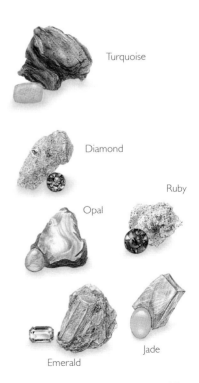
Turquoise

Diamond

Ruby

Opal

Emerald

Jade

Amethyst

Lapis lazuli

male and female sex cell join, the female cell grows into a new individual. Each parent passes on characteristics to its offspring. This process is called heredity.

Heredity works in an amazing way. Inside every cell are tiny

Genetics*: Genes for brown eyes are "dominant"—they dominate over weaker, "recessive" genes for blue eyes. So you have blue eyes only if you inherit two blue-eye genes. Here are the combinations possible in children if both parents have one brown-eye and one blue-eye gene (below) and if one parent has both a blue-eye and a brown-eye gene and the other parent two blue-eye genes (bottom).*

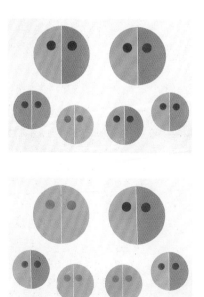

chromosomes, mostly made of the chemical DNA (deoxyribonucleic acid). Different parts of each chromosome carry different "coded messages." Each part is called a gene. The genes carry all the information needed to make a new plant or animal. They decide its sex and what characteristics it inherits. Some characteristics are stronger than others. They are "dominant." Weaker ones are "recessive."

DNA is one of two kinds of nucleic acid—special molecules in cells that play an important part in growth and reproduction. DNA is found only in the nucleus of the cell. RNA (ribonucleic acid) is found throughout the cell, where it controls protein-making.

GENGHIS KHAN
(A.D. 1167–1227)
Genghis Khan was one of the most feared men in history. He was born Temujin, son of a Mongol prince, but became known as Genghis Khan, meaning "conqueror of the world." The Mongols came from central Asia. Wherever Genghis Khan led his Mongol army, terrible tales were told about his cruelty. He conquered many tribes in China, Russia, Afghanistan, and Persia.

GEOLOGY
Geology is the study of the substances that make up the Earth

and of the forces that act upon it to change it. Geologists try to find out what kinds of rocks the Earth is made of and how they got there. They study volcanoes and earthquakes for clues about the underground movements of the Earth. To understand the Earth as it is today, geologists study the history of the planet from its beginnings four billion years ago.

GERMANY

Germany has had a troubled history during this century. It started two devastating wars—World War I (1914–1918) and World War II (1939–1945).

After World War II, Germany split into two. The eastern sector became a communist state—the German Democratic Republic. The western sector was renamed the Federal Republic of West Germany. In 1990, with the collapse of communism, the two became a single country again.

Only northern Germany has a sea coast—on the North and Baltic Seas. Here the land is mainly low and flat. Central Germany is hilly and wooded; in the south there are high mountains and thick forests. In eastern Germany the Elbe and Oder rivers flow north toward the Baltic.

Germany has fertile soil and a mild climate. Farmers grow cereals,

Rainwater trickling down through gaps in the rock is heated by the hot rock beneath.

Geyser

Hot rock

Geyser: In a geyser, steam and superheated water spout into the air through a crack in the rock.

potatoes, and sugar beet, and make wine. They also raise cattle and pigs. The country has lots of timber, iron ore, coal, and hydroelectric power.

See also HITLER; PAGE 60.

GEYSER

A geyser is a spring that spouts hot water and steam into the air from time to time. It is a small sign of the searing heat deep inside the Earth.

A geyser consists of a hole which goes down to a layer of hot rock (usually uncooled lava) and water. When the water is super-heated by the rocks, it erupts or shoots into the air.

Geysers are found in many volcanic regions. The most famous are in Japan, the United States, Iceland, and New Zealand.

See also VOLCANO.

GIRAFFE

The giraffe is the tallest animal in the world. It can reach 20 feet in height. Giraffes live in Africa. They eat leaves, not grass, and when they drink they have to spread their legs wide in order to reach the water. They can run fast to escape from their enemies.

GLACIER

A glacier is a slow-moving river of ice. It flows down the slopes of mountains from an ice cap or high snowfield. Glaciers push stones and boulders along with them. They scrape the soil from the land, smooth the hills, and scour valleys. The rocky mounds piled up by glaciers are called moraines.

During the Ice Ages glaciers spread across the Northern Hemisphere. Boulders carried with the ice can still be seen.

See also ICE AGE; ICEBERG.

GLASS

Glass is a useful material. It is transparent, easy to shape, and cheap to make. It can be made as flat sheets for windows, or into curved lenses for cameras. It can be blown to make bottles, tumblers and other objects.

Glass is made from sand, limestone, and soda ash. These are mixed together and heated in a very hot furnace. They melt and become glass.

Movement of glacier

Moraine

Glacier: *Glaciers carve out U-shaped valleys with flat bottoms.*

GOAT

The goat was one of the earliest animals to be tamed. Its milk, meat, wool, and skin have been useful to people for thousands of years.

The goat is tougher than its relative, the sheep. It can live in dry, rocky country. It climbs well and can eat almost anything. Herds of hungry goats have turned good pastures into deserts. Wild goats live on high mountain crags.

GOLD

Gold is a heavy, yellow metal. It has been used for thousands of years to make jewelry and ornaments because it is beautiful and does not lose its shine. It is also easy to shape. Gold is precious because it is scarce.

Sometimes large lumps of gold, or nuggets, are mined in rocks. But usually gold is found in lodes, or veins in rocks. Half the world's gold is mined in just one part of South Africa.

See also METALS.

GOVERNMENT

People living together in a group need government. They have to agree on what jobs must be done and who should do them.

In a primitive tribe the best hunter or strongest warrior might

Toggenburg

Angora

Goat: The Toggenburg is a domesticated goat from Switzerland. Angora goats are raised for their silky hair. This is made into mohair, a kind of cloth in which angora wool is mixed with cotton or sheep's wool.

become the ruler or chief. The ancient Greeks tried a form of government called democracy, or "rule by the people." The people met to discuss new laws and to decide what taxes should be paid. This was the beginning of the modern parliament.

The president of the United States is head of state and government. Presidents are elected every four years. The U.S. Congress is divided into the House of Representatives and the Senate.

Today every country has a head of state. Britain is a monarchy, so the head of state is the Queen. But the country is ruled by a government of ministers. The head of the government is the prime minister. Parliament is divided into two parts, the House of Commons and the House of Lords.

See also COMMUNISM; DEMOCRACY.

GRASS

Most grasses are slender, with hollow stems and pointed leaves. The plants keep growing even when the leaves are cut.

Cereals are grasses that are also foods. Many farm animals eat grass, fresh in summer and dried as hay in winter. Sugarcane is a kind of grass.

GRAVITY

Throw a ball into the air and it falls back to the ground. This is because the Earth pulls it back. The Earth's pull is called gravity. It is one of the basic forces in the universe. Magnetism is another. Isaac Newton first stated the laws of gravity. He said that every object has an attraction for every other.

Gravity is what keeps all the heavenly bodies in their paths

through space. It keeps the Moon moving in a circle around the Earth. It keeps the Earth moving around the Sun. If there were no gravity, the Moon and Earth would fly off into space.

GREECE AND TURKEY

Greece includes hundreds of islands in the Aegean and Ionian seas. It has natural harbors, mountains and valleys, a rocky landscape of limestone, and a warm, sunny climate. The islands are peaceful, but Greece's cities are busy with people and traffic. In Athens, the capital, air pollution is eating away at its mixture of ancient and modern buildings. Greece's main industries are agriculture and tourism.

Turkey is partly in Europe and partly in Asia. Much of the land is mountainous and dry, but the coastal plains are fertile, with farming as the main industry. Turkey was once the center of the mighty Ottoman Empire that lasted for 500 years but collapsed after World War I.

See also PAGE 60; PAGE 62.

GREECE, ANCIENT

The ancient Greeks built one of the greatest of all civilizations. It began some 4,000 years ago when wandering tribes from central Europe came to the land that we now call Greece.

Over the centuries, Greek civilization developed. Cities were built. Craftsmen made gold ornaments and bronze weapons. Art, music, and poetry developed.

Democracy, "rule by the people," started around 2,500 years ago in Athens. The Athenians also built fine temples and public buildings. For entertainment, the Athenians played music on flutes and lyres or they went to the theater. The Athenians loved to hear stories of great Greek heroes and their deeds. The greatest of these stories were told by the poet Homer in two long poems called the *Iliad* and the *Odyssey*. The beauty of life in Athens can be seen from the ruins that still remain.

Athens was only one of many city-states in Greece. The states quarreled often. The greatest rival of Athens was Sparta, and the two states were very different. Sparta was a military state. Its people were soldiers and the Spartans had no use for art, philosophy, or comfortable homes.

The Greeks were very fond of athletics, such as running, javelin and discus throwing, and wrestling. The first Olympic Games, held in a place called Olympia, took place in 776 B.C. The Greeks had many gods, but the greatest was Zeus, king of the gods.

The age of the city-states in Greece ended in 338 B.C., when King Philip of Macedonia brought all of Greece under his rule.

Greek ideas have survived many centuries, and have been a great influence. The way we live and think today owes a great deal to the civilization of ancient Greece.

GULF STREAM

The Gulf Stream is a very important warm-water ocean current. It is surface water that flows in a clockwise movement

Greece, Ancient: Greek artists carved beautiful sculptures to decorate their public buildings.

around the North Atlantic Ocean. It begins near the equator and drifts past Florida, up the coast of the United States toward Newfoundland, and then moves toward Europe.

Part of the Gulf Stream washes the shores of France, the British Isles, Norway, and Iceland. Because it is warm, winter in these countries is much milder than that of other places as far north.

GUN

Guns are weapons that fire bullets or shells. Small arms, also called firearms, include pistols, revolvers, shotguns, and rifles. Big military guns—artillery pieces —include field guns, howitzers, and mortars.

All guns work in roughly the same way. A gun has a long, hollow, metal barrel. The bore of a gun is the width of the hole in the barrel. One end of the barrel, the breech, is closed; the other end, the muzzle, is open. When the gun is fired, an explosive charge inside a cartridge sends a bullet down the barrel and out of the muzzle with great force.

GUTENBERG, JOHANNES (c.1398–1468)
Gutenberg invented movable type for printing around 1439. His invention meant that books could

be produced cheaply, and that knowledge would be available to many people.

GYMNASTICS
Gymnastics consists of exercises to develop and strengthen the body. There are two main types— Swedish and German. They were developed in the 1800s. Both systems help make people strong, supple, and agile. Gymnasts use equipment such as beams, rings, and horizontal and parallel bars.

Gutenberg: In early printing presses the type was positioned on a wooden base, the paper laid over it, and the wooden screw turned to press the paper onto the type.

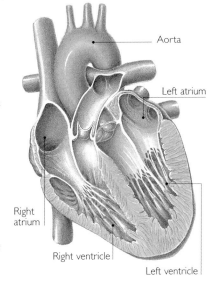

Aorta

Left atrium

Right atrium

Right ventricle

Left ventricle

Heart: *Over the course of an average life, the human heart beats two billion times.*

HANDEL, GEORGE FREDERICK (1685–1759)

Handel was a German-born English composer who was famous for his operas, concertos, and oratorios. His best-known works are the *Messiah*, and *Water Music*.

HANNIBAL (247–183 B.C.)

Hannibal, a general and statesman, was one of ancient Rome's greatest enemies. He came from Carthage in North Africa. In 218 B.C., he invaded Italy by crossing the Alps with his entire army, including war elephants. He fought against the Romans for 15 years but was never able to defeat them.

HARVEY, WILLIAM (1578–1657)

Harvey was an English physician who showed how the heart functioned and proved that blood goes around the body in a circular motion.

HEART

Your heart beats around 70 times every minute. It is a pump—a bag of extra-strong muscle that pumps blood around the body.

The pump is divided into four parts: a left and right atrium above a left and right ventricle. The two sides of the pump work independently. Blood fresh from the lungs enters the left atrium and is forced through a valve down to the left ventricle. From there it is forced into the body's main artery, the aorta, and out of the heart ready to flow around the body.

On the other side, "stale" blood from the body enters the right atrium, passes into the right ventricle, and is forced out toward the lungs, where it will leave its carbon dioxide and pick up vital oxygen.

HEDGEHOG

The hedgehog is one of a group of mammals called insectivores. Although the word insectivore means it eats insects, the hedgehog will eat almost anything. It rolls itself into a prickly ball when frightened and hibernates in winter.

HELICOPTER

A helicopter is a machine that can fly forward, upward, downward, and sideways. This is because it has a rotor, or rotating (turning), wing. Ordinary aircraft have fixed

Rotor blade

Helicopter: A helicopter has spinning rotor blades, which provide both lift and thrust.

wings and their engines can drive them forward only. The helicopter's rotor consists of metal blades mounted on top of the body. Turned by the engine, the rotor screws itself into the air to lift the helicopter off the ground. When a helicopter is flying forward, the rotor blades are angled so that they push the air backward.

HERCULES

Hercules is a hero of ancient Greek and Roman mythology. In a fit of madness, he killed his wife and children. The god Apollo ordered Hercules to perform twelve labors in punishment. Today the word *Herculean* is used to describe an enormous or difficult task.

HIBERNATION

In winter when food is scarce, many animals go into a long, deep sleep. This is called hibernation. During late summer and fall, while food is still plentiful, an animal eats until its body is fat. Then it digs itself into the ground or finds a sheltered place to sleep. While the animal is asleep, its heartbeat and its breathing slows down. It uses so little energy that it can live on the fat in its body.

HIEROGLYPHICS

This was a system of writing used in ancient Egypt. Hieroglyphics began before 3000 B.C. with a very simple kind of picture writing, in which each picture stood for an object. Later, pictures came to represent ideas. Finally, pictures were used to represent sounds in the spoken language.

Hieroglyphics stopped being

Hieroglyphics: *Egyptian scribes used a form of picture writing with about 700 different hieroglyphs.*

used and remained unread until a Frenchman called Champollion deciphered inscriptions on a stone slab, the Rosetta stone, in 1822.

HINDUISM

Hinduism is a religion. Hindus believe that God is present in all things. Their most important holy books are the *Vedas*. Hindu priests, or Brahmans, worship the supreme God. Ordinary people worship lesser gods, such as Vishnu, God of Life.

HIPPOPOTAMUS

The huge hippopotamus lives in the rivers of Africa. Its name means "river horse," but it is actually related to the pig.

Despite their gaping jaws and tusks, hippos eat only plants. They spend the day in the water,

floating or walking along the river bottom, and come ashore at night. Hippos can be dangerous if they are annoyed.

HISTORY

History is the story of the past. Historians are mainly interested in famous people and great events, because these affect nations. But history is also concerned with ordinary people's lives.

Science, medicine, art, religion, and architecture all have histories of their own. History is revealed in many ways: by digging for it, by reading about it in old books and manuscripts, and by listening to people talking.

See the history chart on pages 108–111.

Hinduism: *Shiva is one of the most important Hindu gods.*

B.C.	AFRICA
c.8000	Farming begins
c.4000–3500	Wheel, plow, and sail in Egypt
c.3500	Early writing in Egypt
c.2700–c.2200	Age of Pyramids in Egypt
2050–1800	Middle Kingdom under Theban rulers
670	Assyrians conquer Egypt
525	Persians conquer Egypt
500	Nok civilization founded
332	Alexander the Great conquers Egypt
306	Ptolemy I founds new dynasty in Egypt
30	Death of Antony and Cleopatra. Rome conquers Egypt

A.D.	
100	Kingdom of Ethiopia founded
429–444	Vandals occupy North Africa
533–534	Belisarius reconquers North Africa for Justinian
800s	Civilization of Ghana
969	Fatimids conquer Egypt

B.C.	ASIA
c.6000	Rice cultivation in Far East
c.4000	Farming, plow, wheel in Mesopotamia
c.3000	Civilization of Sumeria
c.2700–1750	Harappan civilization in Indus Valley
c.2000–c.1200	Hittite civilization in Turkey
c.1750–1000	Shang dynasty in China
c.1200–650	Domination of Assyrian Empire
1000–c.500	Chou dynasty in China
551	Birth of Confucius
c.550–330	Achaemenid Empire in Persia
530s	Buddha preaching
334–323	Campaigns of Alexander the Great
c.320–185	Mauryan Empire in India
c.200 B.C.–c.A.D.220	Han dynasty in China
c.6	Birth of Jesus

A.D.	
c.30	Crucifixion of Jesus, founder of Christianity
226–636	Sassanid Empire in Persia
304–308	Huns invade China
c.320	Gupta Empire in Ganges Valley: "Golden Age" of Hindu culture
c.300–500	Main spread of Buddhism in China
c.520	Decimal system invented in India
540	Persian–Byzantine War begins
618–906	T'ang dynasty in China
622	Muhammad founds religion of Islam
636–750	Arabs conquer an empire from Spain to the Indus Valley
794	Japanese capital moves to Kyoto
c.960–1280	Sung dynasty in China
1096	First Crusade

B.C.	EUROPE
c.6500	Farming begins in Greece and the Aegean
c.2000	Bronze Age in north Europe
c.2000–1200	Minoan and Mycenaean civilization in Crete and Greece
753	Rome founded
c.750–c.550	Greeks and Phoenicians colonize Mediterranean and Black Sea
490–479	Battles of the Persian Wars
431–404	Peloponnesian War
c.380–300	Works of Plato, Euclid, and Aristotle
c.327–300	Main Roman expansion
27	Octavian takes title of Augustus: end of Roman republic

A.D.	
c.43	Romans occupy Britain
284–305	Roman Empire reorganized and divided into East and West
313	Freedom of Christian worship in Roman Empire
378	Valens defeated by Visigoths at Adrianople
410	Sack of Rome
496	Baptism of Clovis, king of the Franks
c.600	Slavs move into Balkans
711	Muslims invade Spain
768–814	Charlemagne builds Frankish Empire
800s	Vikings invade and settle northwest Europe
1054	Break between Greek and Roman Churches
1066	Norman conquest
1096–1300	The Crusades

B.C.	THE AMERICAS AND AUSTRALASIA
c.48 000	Aborigines begin to arrive in Australia from Southeast Asia
c.33 000–13 000	People begin to cross the Bering Strait from Asia into North America
c.7000	Agriculture begins in Middle America
c.6000	People living at the southernmost tip of South America
c.1200–100	Olmec tribe of Middle America develop counting system and calendar
c.100	Hopewell tribe of Ohio start to build huge burial mounds, some with bases larger than the Egyptian pyramids

A.D.	
c.300–c.900	Mayan civilization in Central America
c.900	First Maoris arrive in New Zealand
c.1000	Greenland Vikings reach North America
c.1325–1520	Aztec civilization in Mexico

AFRICA	
1250	Mamelukes seize power in Egypt
1300s	Mali Empire in west Africa
1400s–1500s	European settlements on west coast
1500s	Songhai Empire replaces Mali Empire
1652	Dutch found Cape Colony
1869	Suez Canal opened
1880s	"Scramble for Africa"
1899–1902	Boer War
1914	All Africa except Liberia and Ethiopia colonized by European nations
1952–1980	African states win independence
1981	President Anwar Sadat of Egypt is assassinated
1984–1986	Severe famine in East Africa; millions face starvation
1985–1986	Renewed unrest in South Africa results in international pressure for reform of apartheid
1986	U.S. air raid on Libya strikes Tripoli and Benghazi
1990	Namibia becomes independent; in South Africa, African National Congress leader Nelson Mandela is freed from prison after 27 years
1994	The ANC are elected to power in South Africa; Nelson Mandela becomes president; Half a million people are killed during a civil war in Rwanda; more than two million refugees leave the country
1997	President Mobutu is overthrown after a civil war in Zaire; the country is renamed the Democratic Republic of Congo

ASIA	
1192	Yoritomo first shogun in Japan
1206–1280	Mongols conquer empire in central Asia
1368–1644	Ming dynasty in China
1486–1498	Voyages of Bartolomeu Dias and Vasco da Gama
c.1500–1870	African slave trade
1522–1680	Mughal expansion in India
c.1550–c.1650	Russians colonize Siberia
1630s	Japan isolates itself from rest of world
1644–1911	Manchu dynasty in China
1757	Battle of Plassey; British defeat French in India
1805	Beginning of East India Company's dominance in India
1839–1842	Opium War; Britain takes Hong Kong
1857–1859	Indian Mutiny
1867	Shoguns lose power in Japan
1900	Boxer Rebellion in China
1911	Republic established in China under Sun Yat-sen
1937	Japan invades China
1941	Japanese attack Pearl Harbor
1945	U.S.A. drops atomic bombs on Japan
1947	Indian independence
1948	State of Israel founded
1949	Communist victory in China
1957–1973	Vietnam War
1980–1988	Iran–Iraq War
1982	Israel invades Lebanon
1988	In Pakistan Benazir Bhutto becomes first woman Muslim prime minister
1989	Antigovernment demonstrations in Tiananmen Square, Beijing are violently crushed
1990	Iraq invades its neighbor Kuwait
1991	A U.S.-led 29-country coalition attacks Iraq; Iraq surrenders and relinquishes Kuwait
1997	Hong Kong is handed back to China by the British

EUROPE	
1337	Beginning of Hundred Years' War in France
1347–1350	Black Death
c.1450	Gutenberg starts printing
1450–1453	English driven out of France
1453	Constantinople falls to Ottoman Turks
1455–1485	Wars of the Roses
1521	Martin Luther leads Protestant split from Roman Church
1618–1648	Thirty Years' War
1642–1648	English Civil War
1643–1715	Reign of Louis XIV
1750	Start of Industrial Revolution
1756–1763	Seven Years' War
1789	French Revolution begins
1799	Napoleon seizes power in France
1815	Battle of Waterloo; Congress of Vienna
1821–1829	Greek War of Liberation
1848	Year of revolutions throughout Europe
1854–1856	Crimean War
1870–1871	Franco-Prussian War
1885–1895	Daimler and Benz work on automobile; Marconi's wireless
1914–1918	World War I
1917	Bolshevik Revolution in Russia begins
1933	Hitler becomes German chancellor
1936–1939	Spanish Civil War
1939–1945	World War II
1941	Germany invades U.S.S.R.
1945	Defeat of Germany; Cold War begins
1957	U.S.S.R. launches first space satellite; Treaty of Rome: formation of European Economic Community
1989	Communism starts to decline rapidly in eastern Europe
1990	East and West Germany are united
1991	U.S.S.R. breaks up as its republics start declaring their independence
1991–1992	Breakup of Yugoslavia
1995	The U.S.-brokered Dayton peace accord ends war in Bosnia

THE AMERICAS AND AUSTRALASIA	
c.1400–1525	Inca civilization in Andes
1492	Columbus reaches the Americas
1519	Cortes begins conquest of Aztec Empire
1532	Pizarro begins conquest of Inca Empire
1608	French colonists found Quebec
1620	*Mayflower* puritans (Pilgrim Fathers) settle in New England
1642	Tasman discovers New Zealand
1770	James Cook claims Australia for Britain
1776	American Declaration of Independence
1788	British colony founded at Botany Bay, Australia
1840	Britain annexes New Zealand
1846–1848	U.S.A.-Mexico War
1861–1865	American Civil War
1898	Spanish–American War
1911	Mexican Revolution
1914	Panama Canal opened
1917	U.S.A. enters World War I
1929	Wall Street Crash begins Great Depression
1941	U.S.A. enters World War II
1945	United Nations set up
1950	U.S. enters Korean war
1959	Cuban Revolution
1963	President Kennedy assassinated
1969	Neil Armstrong lands on the Moon
1981	First space shuttle flight
1983	U.S. troops invade Grenada
1985	Earthquake in Mexico City claims 5,000 lives
1986	Space shuttle *Challenger* explodes after takeoff; Jean-Claude Duvalier's regime in Haiti is overthrown
1990	U.S. troops overthrow President Manuel Noriega of Panama
1992	Earth Summit held in Rio de Janeiro to discuss environmental protection
1994	U.S.A. lifts 30-year-old trade embargo on Vietnam

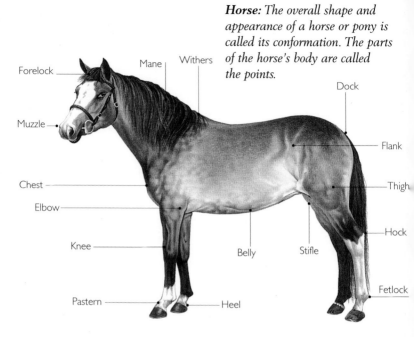

Horse: The overall shape and appearance of a horse or pony is called its conformation. The parts of the horse's body are called the points.

Forelock
Mane
Withers
Muzzle
Dock
Flank
Chest
Thigh
Elbow
Hock
Knee
Belly
Stifle
Pastern
Heel
Fetlock

HITLER, ADOLF (1889–1945)

Hitler became the Führer (leader) of Germany in 1933. He was a dictator whose Nazi party led Germany into World War II. German armies conquered most of Europe and millions of Jews and others were murdered on Hitler's orders. But Britain, the United States, the former U.S.S.R., and their allies defeated the Nazis. To avoid capture, Hitler killed himself.

HOCKEY

Field hockey is one of the most popular games in the world.

It can be played on any smooth, level surface. It is played by two teams of 11 players. The purpose of the game is to hit a small, hard ball with a curved stick into the other team's goal.

Ice hockey was first played as an organized sport in Canada in the late 1800s. It is played on ice with six players, on skates, in each team. Instead of a ball they have a hard rubber disk called a puck.

HOLOCAUST

Holocaust means "a great destruction of life by fire." In recent times the word has been used to refer to the murder of six others by the Nazis in Germany and German-occupied countries before and during World War II. Many of these victims were sent to concentration camps to be tortured, starved, and made to work under horrific conditions before being executed.

HOMER

Two very famous poems called the *Iliad* and the *Odyssey* are said to have been the work of Homer. The poems were written in Greece around 800 B.C. Both poems are about the Trojan War. The *Iliad* tells the story of how the Greeks captured the city of Troy. The *Odyssey* describes the homeward journey of the Greek hero Odysseus.

HORSE

The first horse was an animal no larger than a small dog. It is known as *Hyracotherium*. It had four toes on its front feet and three on its back feet. Gradually over millions of years, the horse evolved, losing all its toes except one, the hoof.

Nobody knows when horses were first tamed. Their first use was to pull war chariots, and cavalry played an important part in wars until early in this century. Horses were the fastest form of transport until the 1800s, when the steam locomotive and the automobile replaced them. Horses were invaluable on farms, where they were used to pull wagons and plows.

Many different types of horses have been bred. Among the largest are the Shire and Clydesdale breeds. The Shetland pony is one of the smallest.

HOVERCRAFT

A hovercraft is often called an air-cushion vehicle because it glides above the ground or water on a cushion of air. The cushion of air is created by a huge fan, which forces air beneath the craft. The air is held there by flaps or skirts around the sides.

Backward-facing propellers on top of the craft steer and propel it forward. The propellers are powered by engines similar to those of an aircraft.

Hovercraft: The hovercraft hovers just above the waves, held up by a cushion of air.

HUMAN BEINGS

People exactly like us have lived for only a few thousand years. We belong to a group of mammals called the primates. Our scientific name is *Homo sapiens*, which means "thinking man."

Fossil remains of our ancestors have been found in Africa and Asia. These early humanlike creatures walked on two legs, and their skulls and teeth were similar to our own. But their brains were much smaller—around the same size as an ape's. After these "ape-men" came creatures much more like modern humans. They had bigger brains and they could use tools. Having a bigger brain made it possible for primitive people to develop until *Homo sapiens* appeared maybe around 100,000 years ago.

The human brain gave human beings the power to hunt, kill, capture, and tame other animals. Human beings developed skills far greater than those of any other creature. They learned to make

Human Body: *The skeleton (left) provides the body with a strong framework, consisting of around 206 bones. Muscles (right) are responsible for movement and are attached to the bones.*

and use fire, to grow food, and to make metal tools. They settled in villages and towns, and used language and writing to store and pass on the knowledge they had gained. In this way, civilization gradually developed.

HUMAN BODY

Our bodies are made of millions of tiny cells, which are grouped together into separate tissues and organs. Skin protects us from heat, cold, injury, and germs. Our bones give us our shape and allow us, with the help of our muscles, to move around.

Our bodies need oxygen and food. We get the oxygen from the air when we breathe. The blood carries the oxygen to every cell of the body. It also carries digested food, which is burned by the oxygen to give us energy.

The body produces lots of waste. Some of this is excreted through the skin when we sweat; some (carbon dioxide) when we breathe out. Other waste is removed via the bowels and the bladder.

The only organs that are different in a man and a woman are the reproductive organs. A woman has a vagina and ovaries which contain ova (eggs). A man has a penis and testes which contain sperm. The fertilization of a female egg cell by a male sperm cell produces one new cell, which

has all the makings of a complete, new human body.

See also BLOOD; BRAIN; BREATHING; CELL; EAR; EYE; HEART; REPRODUCTION; SKIN.

HUMMINGBIRD

Hummingbirds are the smallest birds in the world. Most kinds live in the great forests of South America. Hummingbirds are marvelous fliers. They can hover in midair and even fly backward. Their wings beat so fast they make a humming noise.

Hummingbird: A hummingbird rolls its tongue into a tube to suck nectar from a flower.

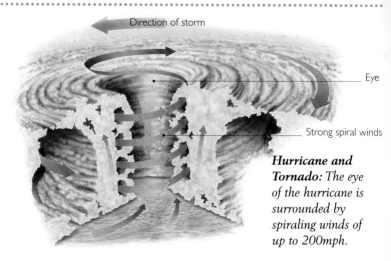

Direction of storm

Eye

Strong spiral winds

Hurricane and Tornado: The eye of the hurricane is surrounded by spiraling winds of up to 200mph.

HURRICANE AND TORNADO

A hurricane is a storm in which the wind circles or spirals inward around a low-pressure area. The winds can be very strong— sometimes more than 200mph— and there is torrential rain, causing floods. Yet the center or "eye" of the storm is quite calm. In the seas off China and Japan, storms like these are called typhoons. In the southern Pacific and Indian oceans, they are called cyclones.

A tornado is a funnel of cloud that sometimes forms on the bottom of a thundercloud, spiraling downward toward the ground. Many tornadoes never reach the ground. But some spin faster, until the winds inside them are going around at 300 mph or so. They hit the ground and leave a trail of destruction.

HYDROFOIL

The hydrofoil is a type of watercraft that has large, winglike structures attached to the hull. As the craft gains speed, the hull rises out of the water on these skilike projections. Because the hull no longer has to push against the water, the craft can travel much faster than an ordinary boat.

HYDROGEN

Hydrogen is an element. It is a colorless gas and has no smell and no taste. It is very light—more than 14 times as light as air.

Atoms of deuterium and tritium, isotopes of hydrogen, can be made to join together at a very high temperature to release huge quantities of energy. This is the principle of the massively destructive hydrogen bomb.

ICE AGE

The Ice Ages were times of intense cold. Sheets of ice spread southward from the North Pole, covering much of Europe, North America, and Asia. The most recent Ice Age ended around 11,000 years ago. Glaciers carried soil and rocks along with them like huge bulldozers. They scraped the land clear of soil and smoothed hills and valleys.

During the recent Ice Age, many plants and animals were killed by the cold. Human beings had to find ways to keep warm. They took shelter in caves and made clothes from the skins of animals. Eventually the ice sheets melted and the weather grew warm again. But it is not certain that in the future there will never be another Ice Age.

See also GLACIER.

ICEBERG

Icebergs are islands of ice that drift in the cold polar seas. They are formed from masses of ice which break off the end of a glacier or ice cap and float off into the sea. An iceberg can weigh millions of tons.

Iceberg: More than 80 percent of an iceberg is submerged beneath the surface of the sea. The tip may rise up to 330 feet above the sea.

Only the tip of the iceberg shows above water. Five times as much is hidden beneath the surface.

See also GLACIER.

ICE HOCKEY

See HOCKEY.

ICE-SKATING

Ice-skating is the sport of gliding across ice on skates, which are metal blades attached to the soles of boots.

People in Scandinavia around 2,000 years ago were probably the first ice-skaters. Today, most people skate in indoor rinks where the ice is specially formed by refrigeration. The sport of ice-skating has three main branches: figure-skating, ice-dancing, and speed-skating. In figure-skating, the skaters make circles, figure eights, and other patterns as they glide across the ice. In ice-dancing they dance on the ice, and in speed-skating they race one another on ice.

IMMUNE SYSTEM

The immune system is the body's way of defending itself against infectious diseases. The bacteria or viruses causing diseases are like invaders. The body fights them off by producing substances known as antibodies, which attack the invaders and gradually overcome them. This is how we recover from infectious diseases.

Sometimes doctors give this process a helping hand through what is known as vaccination. They inject a patient with a vaccine, a very mild form of an infection. The body produces antibodies. After that it is better able to fight off more serious forms of the disease.

See also BACTERIA; DISEASE.

INCAS

Hundreds of years ago the Incas ruled an empire in the Andes Mountains. Its heart was in the South American country we now call Peru. All the people living in the mountain valleys had to work for the Incas. In return, the Incas made sure that everyone had a home and enough to eat.

Incas: *An Inca chief (or* curaca) *holds a special ceremonial vessel during festivities in honor of the Sun god. These were held each year in June.*

The Incas became very rich. In 1532, Spanish explorers came seeking gold. They had horses and guns and they captured the Inca king, Atahualpa. They made themselves rulers of Peru.

INDIA

India is a large country (around 1,270,000 sq. mi.). More than 900 million people live in India. The north is cut off from the rest of Asia by the Himalaya Mountains. Great rivers, such as the Ganges and Brahmaputra, flow across the plains that lie south of these mountains.

Parts of India are dry and hot. It is cooler in the mountains, but most people live in the fertile river valleys. Most of India's rain falls during the monsoon season. Many Indians are poor farmers, who live in small villages. Others live in crowded cities such as Calcutta. Industry is developing in India. There are steelworks, mines, textile and engineering factories.

Most Indians are Hindus, but there are also Buddhists, Sikhs, Muslims, and Christians. Civilization began 4,500 years ago in the area that includes India. From the late 1700s until 1947, most of India was ruled by Britain. Then it became an independent nation.

See also GANDHI; PAGE 62.

INDIAN OCEAN

The world's third-largest ocean covers more than 28,000,000 sq. mi. The Indian Ocean's biggest island is Madagascar, off the coast of Africa. Other islands include Mauritius and the Seychelles. The ocean includes the Bay of Bengal, the Red Sea and The Gulf, known sometimes as the Persian Gulf. In the Indian Ocean's northwestern corner, near the Middle East, its waters are shallow and very warm. In the far south, near Antarctica, they are sometimes close to freezing point.

INDUSTRIAL REVOLUTION

This is the name given to the great change that took place in Europe and America when goods began to be produced in factories. Before that time, many things were made by hand by craftworkers in their own homes. When James Watt harnessed the power of steam in the mid-1700s, all this changed. England's textile industry was revolutionized by the invention of machines that would spin thread and weave cloth. Cities grew as more and more people left farming areas to seek jobs in the factories.

The Industrial Revolution soon spread to the United States. The new factories created wealth. Railroads and canals were built; coal was mined to fuel steam

Industrial Revolution:
*Smoke billows from the
factory chimneys, and
wafts above the
terraced houses
clustered around
the workplace.*

engines and to make steel. The
new wealth was not for
everybody, however. Workers
often lived in crowded conditions
in the towns that grew up around
the factories. They worked long
hours, often for very little pay.
These bad conditions eventually
led to the formation of labor
unions, which fought hard for
better pay and conditions.

INSECT

Insects are found in every part of
the world. There are hundreds of
thousands of different kinds of
insects—including more than
750,000 different types of flies—
but they are all based on a similar

plan. The body
is divided into three
sections. An insect's head
has eyes, jaws, and
antennae, or feelers. The
middle part, or thorax, carries
three pairs of jointed legs and
sometimes two pairs of wings as
well. The end part is called the
abdomen. Some insects get around
by flying; others are amazing
jumpers. A grasshopper can
jump over 2 feet.

Most insects reproduce by
laying eggs. Instead of bones, they
have a hard case that covers the
outside of their bodies. As the
insect grows, it has to shed this
case and grow another.

Some young insects develop
into adults without changing
shape. They are called nymphs.
But many kinds of insects go
through two big changes in shape.
At each stage, the insect looks
different and has a different way

Ladybug

Harlequin longhorn

Great diving beetle

Stag beetle

Brazilian rhinoceros

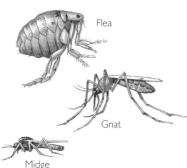

Flea

Gnat

Midge

Insect: *About 80 percent of all known animals are insects, including beetles (above), parasites (left), and flies (below).*

LIFE CYCLE OF A FLY

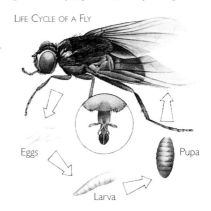

Eggs

Pupa

Larva

of life. Butterflies lay eggs. They hatch into larvae called caterpillars. A caterpillar grows and turns into a pupa, or chrysalis. Finally, the adult butterfly emerges from the pupa. This process of biological change is known as metamorphosis.

Some insects are harmful. Insects such as the mosquito and the tsetse fly carry diseases. The Colorado potato beetle attacks crops. But many insects are useful.

Bees and other insects pollinate flowers. The silkworm makes silk. The ladybug, a kind of beetle, eats greenfly, a garden pest.

See also ANT; BEE AND WASP; BUTTERFLY AND MOTH; PARASITE.

INTERNATIONAL DATE LINE

Geographers have divided the globe into sections with lines that run from pole to pole. These lines are called meridians. Each section is in a different time zone because, as the Earth rotates, the Sun faces different parts of the Earth at different times. The world's nations have agreed that the date changes at the 180th meridian. This imaginary line is called the international date line. Each date begins on the west side of the line and ends on the east side.

INTERNET

The Internet is a huge network in which computers all over the world are linked to each other by telephone lines. Using the Internet people can pass information, including pictures, sounds, and video material, from a computer on one side of the world to a computer on the other. With the correct equipment, anyone, anywhere can link up to it.

A popular Internet service is the World Wide Web, which is a convenient way to steer information around the Internet. Another is E-mail (electronic mail), a way to send messages to other people linked up to the Internet.

INUIT PEOPLES

The Inuit live in the cold Arctic regions. All Inuit once hunted for their food. They traveled in skin

International Date Line: In each of the world's 24 time zones, time differs by one hour from the next. West of the Greenwich meridian it is earlier; east of the meridian it is later. A traveler crossing the international date line in the Pacific Ocean gains or loses a day.

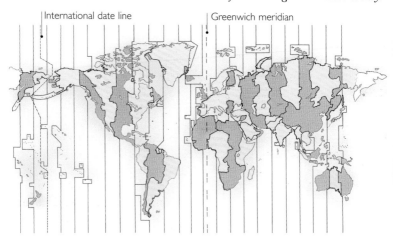

International date line   Greenwich meridian

Iron and Steel:
Molten iron and scrap steel is poured into a furnace, where oxygen is blown into it to raise the temperature and to remove impurities.

canoes, called kayaks, and on sleds. In summer they lived in skin tents and in winter they built igloos. Most Inuit now live in modern towns.

IRELAND
See BRITISH ISLES.

IRON AGE
This is the name given to a period when people began to use iron to make knives, axes, and swords. Iron was first used around 2300 B.C. in Asia Minor. It reached Britain around 500 B.C. The Iron Age followed the Bronze Age.

Iron ores are found in many places in the world and can be smelted (made into iron) fairly simply on charcoal fires.

See also BRONZE AGE.

IRON AND STEEL
Steel is our most important metal. No other metal that is so strong is so cheap. Steel is not a pure metal. It is an alloy made up mainly of iron, together with small amounts of carbon and one or two metals.

Iron by itself is soft and weak, but adding the other ingredients makes it hard and strong.

Steel is like iron in other ways. It is magnetic, and it rusts easily. But by adding metals, such as chromium and nickel, we can make a steel that does not rust. It is called stainless steel.

Iron is found in the form of a mineral, or ore, in the ground. Crude iron is made in a blast furnace by heating iron ore with coke and limestone. Steel is made by purifying the crude iron in other furnaces.

IRRIGATION

Irrigation waters the land to help crops grow. In many places of the world not enough rain falls each year, or it rains only at certain times of the year. Farmers therefore have to get their water from rivers, wells, or lakes.

The ancient civilizations of Egypt, India, China, Assyria, and Babylon depended on irrigation. Today, engineers build dams to make artificial lakes. The water can then be released into pipes, earth channels, or river systems as it is needed.

Shaduf

Canal

Irrigation: Farmers have always practiced irrigation. Simple machines like the shaduf *are used to lift water from a river into ditches. Canals are dug to bring water to dry areas.*

Islam: *Islamic traditions forbid artists to show the face of Muhammad. Because of this, he is often shown with a veil, as in this picture.*

ISLAM

Islam is one of the world's great religions. It was started in A.D. 622 in the Middle East by Muhammad, and today has more followers than any other religion except Christianity. Its followers are called Muslims, and its holy book is the Koran. Muslims believe in one god (Allah) and in Muhammad as his prophet. Islam is widespread in North Africa and the Middle East.

See also MUHAMMAD.

ISRAEL

Israel is a country bordering the Mediterranean Sea in the Middle East. Most Israelis are Jews, and the main language is Hebrew. Many Arabs also live in Israel. Much of the country is hot desert, but farmers grow oranges, cotton, and grain on fertile plains and in fields watered by irrigation. Israel maintains an uneasy peace with its Arab neighbors after conflicts in the 1960s and 1970s.

See also PAGE 62.

ITALY

On the map Italy looks like a boot sticking out into the Mediterranean Sea. The islands of Sardinia and Sicily are also part of Italy. In the north the Alps form a mountain wall between Italy and the rest of Europe.

Southern Italy is warm and fairly dry. In the north it is cooler, with more rain. Both agriculture and industry are important. Most of the factories are in northern Italy. Italy is famous for its wine and for pasta—food such as spaghetti, macaroni, and ravioli.

Most Italians are Roman Catholics. The center of the Catholic Church is the Vatican, a tiny independent state in the middle of Rome. Italy has many old and beautiful buildings. Many of them are in Rome, because 2,000 years ago the Romans ruled Italy. Later, separate city-states grew up. The greatest were Genoa, Florence, and Venice.

J

● ● ● ● ● ● ● ● ● ● ● ● ●

JAPAN

The islands that make up the country of Japan lie off the northeast coast of Asia. The largest islands are Honshu, Hokkaido, Kyushu, and Shikoku. Earthquakes are common and there are volcanoes and hot springs. Japan has heavy rainfall and a cool, temperate climate.

Most Japanese live in cities. Rice, fish, and vegetables are the main foods. There are many factories making all kinds of goods, from cars and ships to radios and zippers.

The Japanese came from mainland Asia around 3,000 years ago. Ancient Japan was ruled by warrior lords. Until the 1850s Japan had little contact with the outside world. But then its rulers decided to allow trade with European countries.

Japan became powerful, and its rulers became warlike. In World War II Japan joined Germany and Italy, and Japanese forces conquered parts of Asia. Japan surrendered in 1945. Today, Japan's emperor no longer has any power. There is an elected parliament and a government led by a prime minister.

See also PAGE 62.

Jellyfish: *A very common jellyfish called* Aurelia *is often washed up on the shore. Up to around 20 inches across, it is easily recognized by the four purplish rings on top. It can sting, but it is not dangerous.*

JEFFERSON, THOMAS
(1743–1826)
Thomas Jefferson, the third president of the United States, was a scholar and thinker as well as a politician. His father was a rich Virginia farmer who gave his son the best possible education. In 1776 it was Thomas Jefferson who wrote most of the Declaration of Independence. He was governor of Virginia from 1779 to 1781. Then he lived for many years in France before returning to America. He was president for two terms from 1801 to 1809. Under him, the United States bought Louisiana from France. After retiring in

1809, he went back to his home, Monticello, where he spent his last years studying and helping to set up the University of Virginia.

JELLYFISH

A jellyfish looks like a transparent umbrella floating in the sea. The body of this sea animal is mainly water. If a jellyfish is stranded on the beach, it dies.

Jellyfish swim by squirting out water from their "umbrellas." They catch small sea animals with stinging tentacles that hang beneath their bodies.

JESUS CHRIST

Jesus Christ was the founder of Christianity. Christians believe that he was the son of God. He taught people to trust in God and lead good, peaceful lives, and he promised eternal life in heaven. He performed miracles, healing the sick and making blind men see again. Jesus' followers said he was

the Messiah. But others feared that he was just a troublemaker. The Romans, who were the harsh rulers of the Jews, also thought so. Jesus was arrested and executed on the cross. But his followers continued to teach others what he had taught them, even though the Romans tried to stop them at first. Many of these early Christians were killed, or martyred, for their belief in Jesus.

JET ENGINE

The jet engine was developed by both Britain and Germany. In 1930, Frank Whittle, a British engineer, patented the first gas turbine for jet propulsion. Germany flew the first successful

Jet Engine: The ramjet is the simplest jet engine. It has neither compressor nor turbine, and is used in missiles. The turbojet is the most common type of engine on commercial airliners.

Ramjet

Turbojet

Turbofan

Turboprop

jet aircraft, the Heinkel 178, in August 1939.

The aircraft gas turbine consists of a rotating shaft with a compressor at the front and a turbine wheel at the back. When the shaft turns, air is drawn into the engine and compressed. It enters combustion chambers, where it mixes with liquid fuel such as kerosene. This mixture burns. The hot gases produced are allowed to escape from the back of the combustion chamber. As the fast jet of gas moves backward out of the exhaust, it thrusts the engine forward.

The jet engine is smaller and lighter than the piston engine, which it has largely replaced. It works efficiently at high speeds and produces great power.

JOAN OF ARC (1412–1431)

In 1429, France was at war with England. Joan was a French girl who believed God told her to save France. She persuaded France's King Charles VII to let her lead his army and, aged just 17, won five battles. But she was captured by the English and burned at the stake as a witch. In 1920, she was made a saint.

JUDAISM

Judaism is one of the world's oldest religions. Its followers are called Jews. They believe in one god, and the Hebrew Bible is their holy book. Christians include the Hebrew Bible in their Bible, calling it the Old Testament. Today, though Israel is their spiritual home, Jews live all over the world.

Joan of Arc: Memorials, such as this stained-glass window, to France's heroine can be seen in churches all over France.

K

KANGAROO

Kangaroos live in Australia. They are the largest of the marsupials, animals that carry their young in pouches.

Kangaroos eat grass and leaves. They travel around in groups called mobs, led by an old male known as a boomer. With their powerful hind legs, and using their long tails to balance them, kangaroos can leap long distances.

KENNEDY, JOHN F. (1917–1963)

John F. Kennedy was the 35th President of the United States. In 1961, he became the first Roman Catholic to be elected to this office. He was also the youngest man ever elected to the presidency. Kennedy was assassinated in Dallas, Texas.

KENYA

Kenya is one of the most beautiful countries in Africa. It has grassland, tropical forests, desert, and the cliffs and ancient volcanoes of the Great Rift Valley.

Kenya's main exports are tea and coffee, and also fruit, vegetables, sugar, cement, and petroleum products.

Some of the most ancient fossil remains of human beings have been discovered in Kenya. From the earliest days of seafaring, traders were attracted there—the Greeks, Portuguese, Romans, and Arabs all built settlements. The influence of Britain spread in the late 1800s, until Britain granted Kenya independence in 1963.

KING, MARTIN LUTHER (1929–1968)

Martin Luther King was a black American minister and leader in the struggle for racial equality in the United States. Because he admired the teachings of Gandhi, he advised people not to use violence when they demonstrated against the segregation of black people.

Kangaroo: *A kangaroo carries its young, called a joey, in its pouch for nearly nine months.*

He won the Nobel Peace Prize in 1964. He was assassinated in 1968 in Memphis, Tennessee.

KING AND QUEEN

In the past, most countries were ruled by monarchs: kings or queens. Usually the king's eldest son succeeded him, which meant that the same royal family might reign for hundreds of years.

English kings ruled with the help of their barons. In 1215 the barons forced King John to sign the Magna Carta, which said that the king should not misuse his powers. Later, English monarchs had to take the advice of parliament. Britain is now a "constitutional monarchy." The Queen is the head of state, but her powers are limited by law. She reigns (holds office), but she does not rule (govern).

King and Queen: *Henry VIII was king of England from 1509 to 1547. He had six wives.*

KINGS AND QUEENS OF ENGLAND SINCE THE NORMAN CONQUEST (1066)	
William I	1066–1087*
William II	1087–1100
Henry I	1100–1135
Stephen	1135–1154
Henry II	1154–1189
Richard I	1189–1199
John	1199–1216
Henry III	1216–1272
Edward I	1272–1307
Edward II	1307–1327
Edward III	1327–1377
Richard II	1377–1399
Henry IV	1399–1413
Henry V	1413–1422
Henry VI	1422–1461
Edward IV	1461–1483
Edward V	1483
Richard III	1483–1485
Henry VII	1485–1509
Henry VIII	1509–1547
Edward VI	1547–1553
Mary I	1553–1558
Elizabeth I	1558–1603

KINGS AND QUEENS OF GREAT BRITAIN FROM 1603	
James I (VI of Scotland)	1603–1625
Charles I	1625–1649
Commonwealth	1649–1660
Charles II	1660–1685
James II	1685–1688
William III and (to 1694) Mary II	1689–1702
Anne	1702–1714
George I	1714–1727
George II	1727–1760
George III	1760–1820
George IV	1820–1830
William IV	1830–1837
Victoria	1837–1901
Edward VII	1901–1910
George V	1910–1936
Edward VIII	1936
George VI	1936–1952
Elizabeth II	1952–

*Dates refer to length of reign.

KIWI

The kiwi is the national bird of New Zealand. It cannot fly, but it waddles around the forest, particularly at night, searching for worms and insects to eat. The kiwi has hairlike feathers, no tail, strong claws, and a long bill. It is the only bird that has nostrils at the tip of its bill.

KNIGHT

A knight in medieval times was a warrior who had vowed to be courageous yet gentle. This code of behavior was called chivalry. A knight gave military service to a lord or an organization such as the church. In return, he was granted land to farm.

The training to become a knight was long and severe. A boy of

Knight: Heavily armored medieval knights on horseback try to unseat each other, in a contest known as a tournament.

noble birth began as a page in the household of another noble family at the age of 7. At 14, he became a squire and began to learn the skills of a knight, such as fighting on horseback. He took vows of knighthood at about 21.

KNOT

A knot is a way to tie rope, string, or thread. We all use knots to tie packages, but many special knots were first developed by sailors to perform different jobs on a sailboat. A bend is used to tie ends of rope together; a hitch is used to tie a rope to a post.

Clove hitch   Reef knot   Bowline   Sheepshank   Two half hitches

Knot: *Choosing the right knot is half the skill of knot tying.*

Common knots are the reef knot, bowline, clove hitch, half hitch, slipknot, and sheet bend.

KOALA

Although it looks like a small bear, the koala is a marsupial. It lives in Australia. Koalas are good climbers. They live in eucalyptus trees, feeding on the leaves.

KORAN

The Koran is the holy book of Muslims. It is believed to have been dictated to Muhammad, the great prophet of Islam, by the archangel Gabriel. It was written down between A.D. 610 and 632.

KREMLIN

The Kremlin is the oldest part of Moscow. It was once the fortress home of the kings, or czars, of Russia. A high wall surrounds the palaces and gold-domed cathedrals of the Kremlin, which is still the seat of the Russian government.

KU KLUX KLAN

The Ku Klux Klan is an organization set up in 1866 by white southerners in the United States to keep newly freed blacks from voting and exercising other rights. Members, dressed in white sheets, beat up and often murdered blacks and public officials. The KKK used violence against both black and white civil rights workers in the South in the 1960s, but it now has little support.

Koala: *A young koala rides on its mother's back after leaving the pouch.*

L

LAKE

Many lakes were formed during the Ice Ages by glaciers scooping out hollows in the land. When the ice melted, the hollows filled with water. Some lakes are artificial—created when dams are built across rivers.

Other lakes are so big that they are called seas. The Caspian Sea in Asia is the largest lake in the world. Its water is salty because the lake has no outlets, and is becoming smaller because of evaporation. The largest freshwater lake in the world is Lake Superior in North America.

See also ICE AGE.

Lake: Lakes form in large hollows in the land. The rivers that flow in and out of most lakes bring mud and sand from other places, so some lakes clog up and disappear.

LANGUAGE

When we speak, we are using language. Language is a collection of "sound signs" or words. We use it to communicate with one another. There are more than 2,800 different languages in the world and many more dialects or local variations. Chinese is the language spoken by the largest number of people. English is spoken in more countries than any other language.

All languages change. People make up new words and often "borrow" foreign words.

LASER

A laser is an instrument that produces a thin beam of very pure light. The beam from some lasers is so powerful that it can blast a hole through metal. Other lasers can be used in surgery to remove or repair diseased body tissue.

An exciting new use of lasers is in communications. Laser beams can carry television signals and telephone messages along glass-fiber tubes. Sending telephone calls by laser is replacing our present telephone system, in which we use copper wires.

LATITUDE AND LONGITUDE

Because we know that the world is round, we can show it on a globe and divide it into sections with accurately drawn lines.

The lines that run east and west and are parallel to the equator are called parallels of latitude. Those that run north and south and pass through the poles are called meridians of longitude.

These lines are measured in degrees. By using these lines we can give the position of any place in the world. Chicago is latitude 41°50'N, longitude 87°45'W.

LAW

All countries have rules that tell people how to behave and which must be obeyed. They make up the law of a country.

Law works differently in different societies. In many countries, groups of men and women are chosen by other people to make the laws. These people are called legislators and the law they make is statute law. Law made by judges is called case law. The law that comes from the customs of the people is called common law.

Lawyers are people who are trained to understand the law. The job of the police and the courts is to arrest and punish people who break the law.

LEAD

Lead is one of the heaviest metals. It is soft, easy to shape, and does not rust. Lead is mixed with other metals to make useful alloys such as pewter, which contains lead and tin. The metal that is used for printer's type contains lead. Solder that is used to join electrical wires and pipes also contains lead. Lead is also used in car batteries.

See also ALLOY.

LEAF

A plant's food is manufactured in its green leaves. Light, water, and carbon dioxide are used to make a form of sugar. From the sugar the plant makes starch and other

Leaf: Leaves, including needles, are the easiest part of the tree to identify. Simple leaves may be rounded, oval, triangular, or long (like willow). They may have toothed or smooth edges, or they may be lobed (like oak).

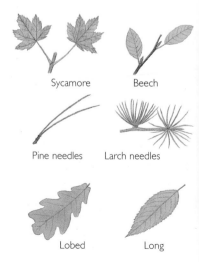

Sycamore

Beech

Pine needles

Larch needles

Lobed

Long

kinds of food that it needs.

The process that makes the food is called photosynthesis. It relies on the green coloring inside a leaf called chlorophyll. The carbon dioxide comes from the air. The water comes from the soil through tiny tubes called veins, and the carbon dioxide enters the leaf through little holes called stomata. The energy for photosynthesis comes from sunlight.

Leaves of most plants growing in mild climates wither and fall off in the fall. Lack of sunlight in winter makes leaves unnecessary. First the water supply to the leaves is cut off. This destroys the green color and gives the leaves red, orange, and brown tints.

LENIN, VLADIMIR (1870–1924)

Lenin is remembered as the man who made Russia a communist country. When he was 17, Lenin decided to work against the Czar (emperor) of Russia, because he thought the Czar's rule was harsh

Lens: Convex lenses (left) make things look bigger, while concave lenses (right) make things look a bit smaller.

and unjust. He became a Bolshevik (Communist) and in 1917 was the leader of the Communist Revolution.

LENS

A lens is a specially shaped piece of a transparent glass or plastic that refracts or bends rays of light. It makes an object look bigger or smaller. A lens that is thicker in the middle is called convex. It makes objects seen through it look bigger. A lens that is thicker at the edge is called concave. Objects seen through it look smaller.

LEONARDO DA VINCI (1452–1519)

Leonardo was a great Italian artist, scientist, and inventor. He was fascinated by the way in which

135

the human body, machines, and the universe work. He designed war engines, a sort of helicopter, a parachute, and diving equipment. His *Last Supper* and *Mona Lisa* are among the most famous paintings in the world.

LEOPARD AND CHEETAH

The leopard lives in Africa and Asia. It is an expert tree climber and sometimes lies in wait for its prey in a tree. It can drag a half-eaten antelope into the branches, out of reach of hyenas.

The cheetah of Africa is the fastest land animal. It hunts by stalking its prey and then chasing it at great speed. Not even the swift antelope can escape, for the cheetah can run at speeds of up to 70 mph, although it can only do so in short bursts.

Leopards and cheetahs both belong to the cat family.

LICHEN

A gray crust can often be seen on rocks and tree trunks. It is made up of tiny plants called lichens. A lichen is really two plants in one. One part is a fungus. The other part is a green plant called an alga. The fungus cannot make its own food. Instead, it takes in water and minerals for the alga. The alga uses the water and sunlight to make food for itself and the fungus.

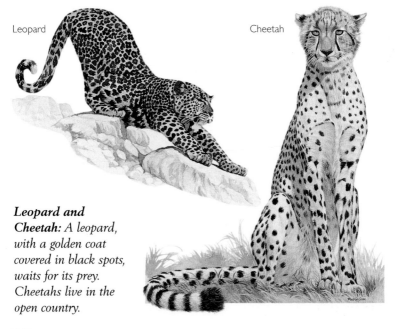

Leopard

Cheetah

Leopard and Cheetah: A leopard, with a golden coat covered in black spots, waits for its prey. Cheetahs live in the open country.

Parmelia caperata

Sea ivory

Cladonia floerkeana

Lichen: *Lichens can survive in some of the hottest and coldest places on Earth. But they particularly favor the clean air of the Arctic and the moist woodlands along Europe's western coast.*

LIGHT

The Sun is a huge furnace that gives out vast amounts of energy as heat and light. Its light is one of the most important things to us on Earth. It enables us to see during the day. We see things because objects reflect light into our eyes. Sunlight also gives green plants the energy to make their food. All animals, including humans, rely on plant food in order to live.

Light travels in straight lines—you cannot shine a flashlight around a corner. But you can reflect the flashlight beam around a corner with a mirror. Light also bends when it passes from air into glass or water. This is called refraction. The bending of light by curved pieces of glass, or lenses, makes it possible to magnify objects, as in the microscope and telescope. When white light is bent by a wedge of glass (a prism), it splits into bands of color. A laser is a powerful beam of very pure light.

See also COLOR; LASER; SUN.

LIGHTNING AND THUNDER

Around 44,000 thunderstorms occur each day, mainly in the tropics. Lightning is a gigantic electric spark that zigzags between the clouds during a thunderstorm.

137

Lightning and Thunder: *Lightning and thunder happen at the same time, but we see lightning before we hear the thunderclap.*

It can also travel down to the ground, where it can cause great damage. It can split trees and set fire to buildings. Tall buildings have to be protected from lightning by a lightning conductor. Lightning may flash in sheets, in balls, or sometimes in forked streaks.

Thunder is produced by the sudden expansion of air that has been heated by the lightning flash. Thunder is heard after a flash because light travels faster than the speed of sound.

LINCOLN, ABRAHAM
(1809–1865)
Lincoln began life poor, but became one of the most famous presidents of the United States. He hated slavery, and led the North to victory against the South in the American Civil War. He was assassinated by John Wilkes Booth, a supporter of the South, in 1865.

See also CIVIL WAR.

LINDBERGH, CHARLES
(1902–1974)
Lindbergh was an American pilot who performed a remarkable feat of daring and endurance. He flew

The flight took 33$\frac{1}{2}$ hours and captured the imagination of the world.

Lindbergh:
Charles Lindbergh
made the first solo nonstop
transatlantic flight in The
Spirit of St. Louis, *a plane*
that he had designed himself.

nonstop in his single-engine plane,
The Spirit of St. Louis, from New
York to Paris in May 1927.

LION
The lion is sometimes called "the king of beasts." With the tiger, it is the largest member of the cat family. Lions live in groups called prides. Only the males have manes. The females, called lionesses, do most of the hunting. Lions feed mainly on antelope and zebras. They creep up on their prey and generally kill it after a short chase. Lions once lived in Europe. Today, wild lions are found only in parts of Africa and in a special reserve in India.

LISTER, JOSEPH (1827–1912)
Lister was an English surgeon who did many things to make operations safe. He used phenol to clean instruments and to kill

Lion: A lion and
lioness doze in
the African sun.
They can sleep
for more than
18 hours a day.

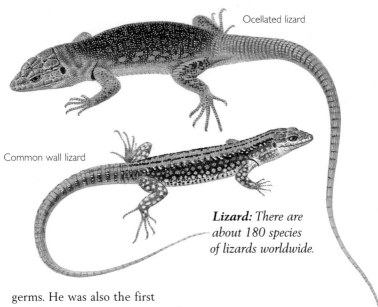

Ocellated lizard

Common wall lizard

Lizard: There are about 180 species of lizards worldwide.

germs. He was also the first person to use catgut in surgery for stitching wounds.

LIZARD

Lizards are reptiles. Most lizards have four legs, but some are legless. The slowworm has no legs. Unlike snakes, lizards have movable eyelids and visible ears.

Lizards generally live in warm climates. Most kinds lay eggs, but some produce live young. Lizards feed on insects, small mammals, or plants. They prefer dry land, but the marine iguana is a good swimmer.

See also REPTILE.

LLAMA

The llama looks like a small woolly camel without a hump. This hardy creature lives in the Andes Mountains of South America.

Llamas are useful because they can carry loads along narrow mountain tracks. They also provide people with meat, wool, skins for making leather, and fat for candles.

LUTHER, MARTIN (1483–1546)

Luther was a monk who thought the Roman Catholic Church had moved too far away from the teachings of the Bible. He also objected to the custom of selling people pardons for their sins. Many Christians agreed with Luther. They started a great religious movement—the Reformation—which resulted in the formation of the Protestant churches.

M

MACHINES, SIMPLE

Machines are devices that put
energy to work. Most machines
are complicated devices, but they
are all based on six types of
simple machine: the lever; the
inclined plane; the wheel and
axle; the pulley; the wedge; and
the screw (see illustrations).

Starting from these simple
machines, engineers have
developed machines that can
do a vast range of things. All
machines, whether a simple lever
or a giant crane, make it possible
for people to do things more
quickly and easily than they
could by hand.

Pulley

Screw jack

Inclined plane

Block
and
tackle

Lever

Wedge

Wheel and axle

Machines, Simple: *Six of the
illustrations on this page show the
simplest possible machines. You may
not realize it, but you see some of
them every day. The seventh, the
block and tackle, is used to lift heavy
weights. The more wheels that are
used, the easier the lifting is.*

MAGELLAN, FERDINAND
(1480–1521)

Magellan was a Portuguese navigator in the service of Spain. He sought a sea route westward to the Moluccas, where spices were grown. He set out with four ships, found the route to the Pacific through what he named the Magellan Strait, and went on to the Philippines, where he was killed. One of his ships completed the first voyage around the world in 1522.

MAGIC

Before people understood what caused such things as storms or disease, many thought that nature was controlled by good and evil spirits. They believed that magic gave them power over these spirits. Some magic was good, or "white;" but other magic was bad, or "black." The clever tricks of stage magicians and conjurers today really have nothing to do with magic.

MAGNET

Magnets can pick up, or attract pieces of metal, particularly iron and steel. This power is called magnetism. Magnetism is most powerful at the ends of the magnet. If you hang a bar magnet by a thread, it always points its ends toward the Earth's north and south magnetic poles. So we call

Magnet: *Both the north and south poles of a horseshoe magnet can be used to pick up an object. The invisible lines of magnetic force stretch out between the two poles.*

the two ends its north and south poles. The magnet always points north–south because the Earth itself acts like a giant magnet. One magnet affects another. The needle in a compass is a magnet.

MAMMAL

Mammals are the most advanced animals. They are vertebrates (animals with backbones) and are warm-blooded. They can control the temperature of their bodies by sweating or panting when it is hot, and shivering when it is cold. Because of this, mammals can live in both hot and cold climates. They usually have hairy or furry skins.

Almost all mammals, including human beings, give birth to live young, rather than eggs. The female feeds the young with milk from her body, and cares for

them until they can take care
of themselves.

Mammals range in size from
tiny shrews to huge whales. Most
mammals are land animals, but
dolphins and whales spend all
their lives in the sea.

MAMMOTH

The mammoth was a hairy
elephant. It lived during the
Ice Age but is now extinct.
Mammoths had long wooly hair
and a thick layer of fat to keep
out the cold. Prehistoric people
hunted mammoths for food and
sometimes drew pictures of
them inside caves.

MAO TSE-TUNG (1893–1976)

Modern China was founded by a
farmer's son, Mao Tse-tung. He
led the peasants in a revolution
that changed China's government
and way of life. He became a
communist, and for many years
the communists fought against the
government. Mao was their leader,
and in 1949 he led his armies to
victory. China became a
communist state.

See also COMMUNISM.

MAPS AND GLOBES

A map is a drawing that shows
all or part of the Earth's surface. It
can show how cities, roads,
railroads, rivers, mountains,
forests, and other features are
arranged on the land.

A flat map cannot be entirely
accurate because the Earth is
round. Maps are drawn by various
methods called projections. A
globe is like a ball with a map of
the world drawn on it. Globes are
more accurate than flat maps, but
less convenient.

Maps are drawn to scale. For
example, a distance of one inch on
the map may represent ten miles
on the ground itself.

Political maps show countries,
and often cities, roads, and
railroads as well. Physical maps
show mountains, rivers, and
other land features.

Mammoth: The now-extinct
wooly mammoth, with its
inward-curving tusks, was closely
related to the modern elephant.

MARCO POLO (*c.*1254–1324)

The book, *The Travels of Marco Polo*, recorded the adventures of this Venetian merchant. With his father and his uncle he journeyed to China in 1275. The emperor, Kublai Khan, favored Marco and made him first a court attendant and later an official. He served the emperor for 17 years. They returned home in 1295, bringing with them great wealth.

MARCONI, GUGLIELMO (1874–1937)

Marconi was an Italian, who worked with, and made important discoveries

Marconi: An early Marconi radio set, with loud-speaker and headphones. In a modern radio, the glass valves have been replaced by transistors.

about, radio waves. He patented wireless telegraphy. In 1901, he sent the first wireless message across the Atlantic.

MARX, KARL (1818–1883)

Marx was the founder of the modern communist movement. His writings greatly changed the way many people thought about society. He helped to write *The Communist Manifesto* in 1848, arguing that all old forms of government had to be overthrown. In *Das Kapital* he wrote that working people should rule and run the factories.

MATHEMATICS

Mathematics is a science that deals with numbers and shapes. Arithmetic is one branch of mathematics. The other main branches are algebra, geometry, trigonometry, and calculus. Arithmetic deals with figures. Algebra deals with figures and symbols. Geometry deals with shapes. Trigonometry deals with the measurement of triangles and the problems associated with this. Calculus deals with changing quantities.

MATTER

All solids, liquids, and gases are matter. Matter is anything that takes up space, responds to the force of gravity, and stays still

Maya: The Maya of Central America built massive pyramids and were the only ancient people in the Americas to develop writing and an accurate calendar.

unless acted upon by an outside force. We can see, hear, touch, taste, or smell some kinds of matter, and measure it. These qualities distinguish matter from things that are mental, like ideas, or like love or hate.

MAXWELL, JAMES CLERK
(1831–1879)
James Clerk Maxwell was a scientist who made important discoveries about electricity and magnetism. Born in Scotland, he was educated in Edinburgh but later moved to Cambridge University in England, where he became a professor. Long before the radio was invented, he was one of the first people to suggest that radio waves must exist. He was also interested in color and light and produced one of the first color photographs, using the three-color process.

MAYA
The Maya Indians developed a civilization in Central America from the 5th century. They built great cities of stone, with palaces, temples, pyramids, and observatories. The Maya were astronomers and mathematicians, and they developed an advanced kind of writing. Like the other early civilizations in the Americas, they never developed the wheel. They did not have metal tools until late in their history, and most of their great engineering feats were accomplished using stone tools. Descendants of the Maya still live on and near the Yucatán Peninsula.

MAYFLOWER

The *Mayflower* was the ship that brought the Pilgrims from Plymouth, England to Massachusetts in 1620. Persecuted for their Puritan beliefs, this intrepid band planned to start a settlement in Virginia, but storms blew the *Mayflower* off course. After more than two months at sea, the settlers reached what is now Cape Cod. They crossed Cape Cod Bay and founded the colony of Plymouth in December 1620.

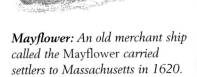

Mayflower: *An old merchant ship called the* Mayflower *carried settlers to Massachusetts in 1620.*

MEASUREMENT

How long is your desk? How heavy are you? How much water is in the bottle? We find the answers to these questions by measuring. We measure by using devices or instruments marked with a scale of numbers. To measure length we use a rule. For weight, we use a pair of scales. For volume, we use measuring cups.

Although the numbers on the scales may be the same, they mean different things. On the ruler, 12 may mean 12 inches; on the pair of scales, 12 pounds; and on the pitcher, 12 fluid ounces. The inch, pound, and fluid ounce are different units of measurement. They are units of length, weight, and volume in the imperial system of measurement.

In the metric system, the units go up in steps or multiples of ten. It was devised in France in the late 1700s and has been used in the majority of Europe for most of the 1900s.

MEDICI FAMILY

The Medicis ruled the city-state of Florence in Italy for 300 years during and after the Renaissance. They made it into a prosperous and beautiful city and built magnificent palaces and churches. Two of the most famous of the Medici rulers were Cosimo (1389–1464) and Lorenzo the Magnificent (1449–1492). The last of the Medicis to rule died in 1737.

MEDICINE

Since very early times people have searched for medicines to heal wounds and cure diseases. The first drugs came from berries and herbs that had healing powers.

The ancient Greeks and Romans knew what the inside of the human body looked like. But they did not know how the different parts worked, or what made them go wrong.

Medicine made little progress until the 1600s, when doctors began studying anatomy (the parts of the body). By cutting up dead bodies, they began to find out

how the body works. As nobody knew about germs, doctors did not worry about cleanliness. Many patients died because hospitals were dirty places.

Over the next 200 years, progress in medicine was slow. But in the 1700s, vaccination was discovered as a way of preventing disease, and later, antiseptics were developed to kill harmful germs. Anesthetics came to be used to deaden pain during operations. In the 1900s the discovery of X-rays meant that doctors could examine the insides of their patients without cutting them open. Powerful new drugs called antibiotics were also discovered.

See also DISEASE; DRUGS; X-RAY.

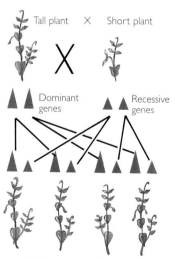

Tall plant × Short plant

Dominant genes

Recessive genes

All offspring are tall

Mendel: By crossing tall plants with short ones, Mendel showed that tallness is dominant over shortness, because all the offspring were tall.

MENDEL, GREGOR (1822–1884)

Mendel was an Austrian monk who studied the way physical characteristics are passed on from parent to child. He observed that

147

Meteor: Meteors usually burn up around 30 miles above Earth. Anything larger than a stone will light up the sky like a fireball. It may hit the ground as a meteorite.

the color and shape of peas were passed on from one generation to the next according to certain laws.

His discoveries went unnoticed until improved microscopes made it possible to see chromosomes, the minute threadlike bodies that carry these hereditary characteristics.

See also GENETICS.

METAL

There are more than 60 different metals. They form the most important group of elements. They are very different from the other elements. Metals pass on, or conduct, electricity and heat well. Most nonmetals do not. Many metals have a silvery, shiny surface. They are tough and strong, but can be bent and hammered without breaking.

Most metals are found in the form of mineral ores. They must be separated before they can be used. There are several different ways of taking, or extracting, a metal from its ore. Iron is extracted by smelting aluminum, by means of electricity.

Metal may be shaped by casting, hammering, rolling, forcing through holes, and cutting.

See also ALUMINUM; COPPER; GOLD; IRON AND STEEL; MINING.

METEOR

On some nights you may see bright streaks in the sky. Though they look like falling stars, these glowing trails are actually made by meteors, lumps of rock, or metal. As they shoot through the upper part of the Earth's atmosphere they burn up in a flash of light.

MEXICO

Mexico is a republic and lies just south of the United States. Most of it consists of a broad, central plateau that is flanked on both sides by mountain ranges. On the west is the Pacific Ocean and, on the east, the Gulf of Mexico and the Caribbean Sea. There are three main kinds of climate—cool, temperate, and hot—and a huge variety of plant life.

Over a third of Mexico's 93 million people work on the land, growing mostly corn, beans, coffee, cotton, sugar, and vegetables.

Michelangelo: This great Italian sculptor and painter carved a huge statue of Moses for the tomb of Pope Julius II.

Mexico is rich in minerals. Its silver and gold originally attracted the Spanish. There is also oil. Mexico's factories produce a wide variety of goods.

MICHELANGELO (1475–1564)

Michelangelo was a sculptor, architect, painter, and poet who lived in Italy during the Renaissance. Among his most famous statues are the *Pietà* and *David*. He painted a scene on the ceiling of the Sistine Chapel in the Vatican depicting the creation of the world.

See also RENAISSANCE.

MICROSCOPE

A microscope makes small objects look bigger, so that we can see things that are invisible to the naked eye.

Ordinary microscopes magnify by bending light rays with glass lenses. The bent rays make an image that is bigger than the original object. Electron microscopes are much more powerful than ordinary microscopes, and can magnify things hundreds of thousands of times. They magnify by bending beams of electrons, rather than light rays.

See also LENS; LIGHT.

Microscope: An optical microscope has a base, a tube containing the lenses, and a body, or upright, to hold the tube.

Eyepiece

Adjustment knobs

Lenses

Stage

Mirror

MIDDLE AGES

The Roman Empire fell in A.D. 476 and it took 1,000 years for strong nations to grow out of the confusion that followed. In between lay the Middle Ages. In the early Middle Ages, Europe was overrun by barbarians. They sacked and burned towns, and soon the art and learning of Rome and the classical world was forgotten, except by monks.

To defend themselves, people banded together under the protection of strong leaders, or kings. The peasants became the vassals of rich nobles and knights. They traded crops and services for protection. The nobles became vassals of the king. In return for the king's protection, they promised to supply soldiers in war. This is known as the feudal system.

Life in the Middle Ages was often harsh and cruel. Any person who broke the law was severely punished. And anyone who questioned the Church's teachings was also punished harshly. But slowly knowledge grew.

Universities and schools were founded, and beautiful cathedrals were built. Gradually government became more settled, and trade flourished. With the voyages of discovery in the 1400s and the Renaissance, the Middle Ages came to an end.

Middle Ages: Many medieval towns held a market once or twice a week. The town square was filled with bustling crowds and traders shouting their wares.

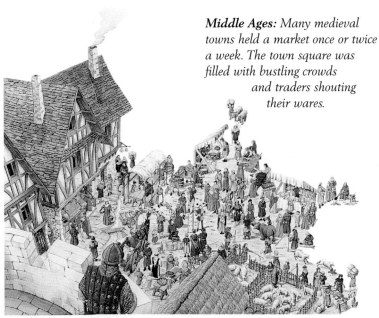

MIDDLE EAST

The desert lands of southwest Asia and northeast Africa are often called the Middle East. This area stretches from Egypt to Iran. Most of the people are Muslim Arabs. Many are poor, but oil fields have made some Middle East countries rich.

In 1948 the Jews founded the independent state of Israel in what had been British-ruled Palestine. The Arabs would not accept this. As a result, there have been five wars between Israel and the Arab countries—in 1948, 1956, 1967, 1973, and 1982.

See also PAGE 62.

Quarry
Open-cast mine
Mine shaft

Mining: Thousands of years ago, our ancestors began mining flint to shape into tools and weapon heads. Since then we have discovered many uses for the Earth's rock and mineral resources.

MIGRATION, ANIMAL

Many swallows spend the summer in Europe. But in the fall they fly south to the warmth of Africa. This journey is called migration.

Many animals migrate to find food or to breed. Caribou move south to escape the Arctic winter. African antelope migrate during the dry season to find water and fresh grass. Frogs, toads, and newts spend most of their time on land. But they return to ponds and streams to lay their eggs.

MINERAL

A mineral is any substance that can be mined. There are nearly 3,000 kinds of minerals. Some, such as gold and silver, are pure

elements. But most, such as salt and coal, are combinations of the 92 naturally occurring elements. Pure minerals are made up of atoms arranged in regular patterns known as crystals. This is what makes jewels like diamonds and emeralds sparkle.

See also GEM; MINING.

MINING

Mining is taking minerals from the ground. It is one of our most important industries and supplies many other industries with their raw materials.

Sometimes mineral deposits can be dug out from the surface. Other deposits lie just below the surface.

The soil is first stripped away, then explosives break up the deposits.

Often the mineral deposits are buried deep in the ground. Miners have to travel by elevator down shafts and in trains along tunnels to reach them.

MISSILE

A missile can be anything that is thrown or fired at a target. Today the word usually refers to a military weapon that has an automatic control system. Many are powered by a rocket engine and carry an explosive warhead. A guided missile is controlled by radio or radar and stays within the Earth's atmosphere. A ballistic missile goes beyond the atmosphere under rocket power, but returns to Earth in an unguided path called a ballistic trajectory.

MOLLUSK

Mollusks are animals with soft bodies. To protect themselves, many mollusks have shells.

Some mollusks, such as the mussel, stay inside their shells and hardly ever move. Others—the cockle, for example—use their single foot to move around.

Slugs and snails are mollusks but slugs have little or no shell. They crawl very slowly. Slugs and snails are garden pests, eating

Mollusk: The brown-lipped snail is a land-dwelling mollusk, with eyes at the tips of its longer tentacle.

young and low-lying plants. The largest and most active mollusks are the octopus, which has no shell, and the squid, which has its shell inside its body.

MONASTERY

A monastery is the home of a religious community. The monks who live in the monastery take vows promising not to marry, not to have possessions or money, and do whatever work they are asked to do. They spend the day working, studying, or in prayer. Some monks work outside the monastery as missionaries and teachers. The long tunic many monks wear is known as a habit.

The first Christian monasteries were started around 200 years after the death of Christ.

Money

Originally, people did not use money. They bartered or traded. When people settled in towns, trade became more complicated. The barter system was too clumsy. So token goods, such as cattle or shells, were used. This was the beginning of the money system.

Later, small pieces of metal, or coins, came into use. The first were made just before 600 B.C. in Asia Minor. Governments issued coins, using gold, silver, bronze, copper, and other alloys. They made them in a place called a mint.

Merchants in the Middle Ages began to exchange pieces of paper, promising payment for goods bought. They set up banks, in which to keep their gold safe. The banks began to issue paper money, or banknotes, and people gradually accepted that these had the same value as gold.

Today, the government controls how much money is made by minting coins and printing notes. The money we use is token money; that is, modern coins are made of cheap metals and have little value in themselves. The real value of money is the number of things it will buy.

Monkey

Monkeys belong to the group of animals called primates. Old World monkeys live in Africa and Asia.

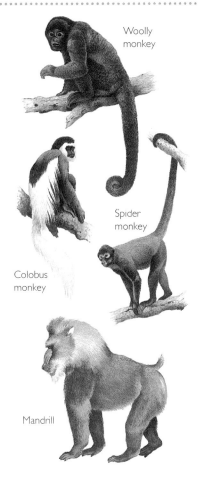

Monkey: The colobus and mandrill are both Old World monkeys, living in Africa. New World monkeys include the spider and woolly monkeys.

New World monkeys live in Central and South America. New World monkeys have prehensile tails that can grasp a branch like

153

an extra hand. Old World monkeys cannot do this.

Monkeys are lively, intelligent animals. They use their hands and feet to hold things. Most monkeys live in groups. They eat fruit and other parts of plants, insects, small mammals, and birds' eggs.

MOON

The Moon is a ball of rock, about a quarter the diameter (width) of the Earth. It has no atmosphere. Because there is no air, there is no weather on the Moon, and no sound. There is no water and no life at all. It is very hot in the sunlight, but icy cold when in the shade.

The Moon's surface is not smooth. There are great, flat plains, and jagged peaks and mountain ranges. Everywhere on the Moon there are pits, or craters. The whole surface is covered with loose rocks and a thick layer of fine dust.

The Moon travels around the Earth once every 27 days. The shape of the Moon appears to change during the month, but what changes is the area we can see which is lit by the Sun. This area changes because of the Moon's movement around the Earth.

See also ECLIPSE.

Moon: *The Earth-turned face of the Moon (top) has many lava plains or maria; the far side (below) is cratered.*

MOSES

Moses was one of the most important leaders of the ancient people of Israel. He lived more than 3,000 years ago. According to the Bible, the Israelites had become slaves of the Egyptians. The Old Testament tells how God appeared to Moses in a burning bush and told him to bring his people to freedom. Moses led them through the Red Sea, whose waters parted to let them pass, then rolled back down again to drown the pursuing Egyptians. Later, God gave Moses the Ten Commandments, the laws that are still the basis of much Jewish and Christian teaching.

MOSQUE

Mosques are the buildings in
which the services of the Islamic
religion take place. Most mosques
have a dome, a minaret, from
which the faithful are called to
prayer five times a day, and a
prayer niche showing the
direction of Mecca.

MOSS

Mosses are simple plants. They do
not have flowers, but reproduce
by sending out tiny offshoots.
Spores, or cells, grow on these
shoots. When the spores are ripe,
they are blown away by the wind.
New moss plants develop from
them.

MOTION PICTURE

See FILM.

MOTORCYCLE

A motorcycle is a vehicle that has
two, and sometimes three, wheels.
The first motorcycles were built
at the end of the 1800s when men
such as Edward Butler, an
Englishman, and Gottlieb
Daimler, a German, started
making powered bicycles and
tricycles. The first motorcycle
races in 1907 encouraged
improvements in design, which
soon brought the motorcycle to
something like its present form—
electric ignition, variable gears,
and the engine mounted low
down between the two wheels.

MOUNTAIN

Mountains are masses of rock that
rise at least 2000 feet above the
surrounding land.
Mountains are usually
grouped together in ranges,
chains, or massifs. Some
mountains are the cones of
volcanoes. But most are
formed by folding and
sideways movements of the
crust, or outer skin, of the Earth.
These movements push up the
rocks to build mountains.
Creating a mountain
takes millions of years.
It is still happening
today in parts of the
Earth. The rocks are
worn away by rain,
wind, ice, and snow.

*Motorcycle: The
Honda VF400 is both
lightweight and powerful.*

155

HIGHEST MOUNTAINS

Asia	Feet
Everest	29,028
K2	28,250
Kanchenjunga	28,208
Makalu	27,790
Dhaulagiri	26,810
Nanga Parbat	26,660
Annapurna	26,494
Gasherbrum	26,471
Gosainthan	26,291
Nanda Devi	25,648
South America	
Aconcagua	22,835
North America	
McKinley	20,320
Africa	
Kilimanjaro	19,341
Europe	
Elbruz	18,482
Mont Blanc	15,771
Antarctica	
Vinson Massif	16,861
Oceania	
Wilhelm	15,401

The height of a mountain is always measured in height above sea level. The world's highest mountains are in the Himalayas in Asia. Mount Everest (29,028 feet) is the highest.

MOZART, WOLFGANG AMADEUS (1756–1791)

The Austrian composer Mozart was a musical genius. He began writing music at the age of five. Two years later his father took him to play at concerts in the great cities of Europe. Mozart wrote church music, opera, and nearly 50 symphonies. He worked hard but earned little money and died very poor at the age of 35.

MUHAMMAD (A.D. 570–632)

The Arab prophet Muhammad founded the religion of Islam. He taught people to stop worshiping idols and follow the "true God," called Allah. In 622, Muhammad's enemies drove him out of his birthplace, Mecca. He fled to the city of Medina, and converted many people to the new religion. By the time Muhammad died, Islam had spread throughout the Arab world.

MUSHROOM AND TOADSTOOL

These plants belong to the fungus group. Fungi are not green. They contain no chlorophyll, so they cannot use sunlight to make their food, like other plants. Instead they feed on dead and decaying plant and animal matter. Some are parasites. Fungi have no flowers or seeds and reproduce by means of cells called spores, which are carried by the wind.

See also PHOTOSYNTHESIS.

MUSIC

Music is a set of sounds arranged in a way that is pleasant to hear. It has rhythm (the beat), harmony (the total sound when several notes are

Death cap

Chanterelle

Ugly milk cap

Lawyer's wig

Mushroom and Toadstool: Some of these fungi are extremely tasty; others are deadly poisonous.

Mozart, Beethoven, and Brahms. They wrote symphonies (long pieces of music for orchestras) and chamber music (for smaller groups of instruments). They also wrote music for choirs. Some composers have written operas— musical plays in which all the words are sung.

FAMOUS COMPOSERS

Antonio Vivaldi	Italian (?1678–1741)
Johann Sebastian Bach	German (1685–1750)
Wolfgang Amadeus Mozart	
	Austrian (1756–1791)
Ludwig van Beethoven	German (1770–1827)
Franz Schubert	Austrian (1797–1828)
Hector Berlioz	French (1803–1869)
Frédéric Chopin	Polish (1810–1849)
Robert Schumann	German (1810–1856)
Franz Liszt	Hungarian
	(1811–1886)
Giuseppe Verdi	Italian (1813–1901)
Richard Wagner	German (1813–1883)
Johannes Brahms	German (1833–1897)
Peter Ilyich Tchaikovsky	Russian (1840–1893)
Antonín Dvořák	Czech (1841–1904)
Edvard Grieg	Norwegian
	(1843–1907)
Edward Elgar	British (1857–1934)
Giacomo Puccini	Italian (1858–1924)
Gustav Mahler	Austrian (1860–1911)
Claude Debussy	French (1862–1918)
Jean Sibelius	Finnish (1865–1957)
Sergei Rachmaninov	Russian (1873–1943)
Béla Bartók	Hungarian (1881–1945)
Igor Stravinsky	Russian (1882–1971)
Dmitri Shostakovich	Russian (1906–1975)

played together), and usually melody (the tune). Music is made up of notes that may be long or short, loud or soft, high or low.

At first, music had a simple melody and rhythm. But it gradually grew more complicated. Two or three tunes were played together. This rich sound was called counterpoint.

People who make up music and write it down are called composers. Two great composers of counterpoint were Bach and Handel. A lot of great music has been written for orchestras by composers such as Haydn,

157

People often call this kind of music "classical" music. There are many other kinds of music, including folk, jazz, and pop music. Modern music is very different from the music of the 1800s. It has difficult rhythms

***Musical Instrument:** In the Western orchestra, instruments are arranged into families of strings, woodwind, brass, and percussion.*

Flute

Trumpet

Clarinet

Violin

French horn

Kettledrum

Harp

Tubular bells

Cymbals

and sounds, and sometimes requires electronic instruments as well as wind, stringed, and percussion instruments.

See also BACH; BEETHOVEN; MOZART; OPERA.

MUSICAL INSTRUMENT

Musical instruments have been made for thousands of years. There are three main groups of instruments. Wind instruments are played by blowing down a hollow wooden or metal tube with holes cut in it. By covering some holes with the fingers, different notes are produced. Wind instruments include flutes, clarinets, trumpets, and horns.

The stringed instruments have strings stretched across a hollow box. The strings are bowed, like a violin, or plucked, like a guitar, to make different notes. Short strings make high notes and long strings make low notes. Stringed instruments include violins, guitars, banjos, and lutes.

Instruments such as drums, cymbals, and bells, which are hit with hammers or sticks, are called percussion instruments.

See also ORCHESTRA.

Mythology: In one of the great ancient Greek myths, Perseus turned the court of King Polydectes to stone by holding up the hideous head of Medusa.

MYTHOLOGY

Mythology is the study of the myths, or stories, that ancient peoples told about their creation and origins, their gods and goddesses. The most familiar to us are the myths created by the ancient Greeks and Romans. Myths were a part of their religion, for they believed that many gods and goddesses inhabited the Earth—gods of the Sun and Moon, gods of war, of the sea and forests, of rain and thunder. The Greek gods lived on Mount Olympus, and the stories told about them were full of heroic adventures and amazing feats. The Greek poets Hesiod and Homer recorded many of these myths in writing. The Romans adopted many of the Greek myths and told dramatic stories about their own gods and heroes that were similar to the Greek myths.

The Norse people of Scandinavia also developed a rich mythology.

N

NAPOLEON BONAPARTE (1769–1821)

After the French Revolution in 1789, Napoleon conquered much of Europe. In 1804 he made himself Emperor of France. But in 1812 his army had to retreat from Russia, and the British and Prussians beat the French at the Battle of Waterloo in 1815. He was exiled, and died on the island of St. Helena.

NASSER, GAMAL ABDUL (1918–1970)

Nasser was an Egyptian revolutionary and army officer. He helped to depose King Farouk in 1952 and became president in 1956. He tried to modernize Egypt. In 1956 he nationalized, or took over, the Suez Canal.

Napoleon: Napoleon's greatest victory was at the Battle of Austerlitz, where he defeated a combined force of Austrians and Russians in 1805.

NELSON, HORATIO (1758–1805)

Nelson was a great British admiral, whose statue stands in the center of Trafalgar Square, London.

He fought and defeated the French fleet led by Napoleon near Alexandria in 1798 (the Battle of the Nile). His most famous battle was at Trafalgar in 1805. He was shot and killed during this battle.

NATIVE AMERICAN

Native Americans were the first peoples in North America. Scientists believe that they came from Asia between 15,000 and 35,000 years ago. They crossed the land that then connected Asia with Alaska, and moved southward.

There were hundreds of tribes, each with its own customs and way of life. Some tribes lived by hunting and food-gathering, and others were farmers and fisherman.

When the first Europeans came to North America, relations with

Native American: The tepee, the traditional home of Plains tribes, is a cone-shaped tent made from skins and bark and supported by poles.

Native Americans were friendly. But as Europeans settled the continent, the Native Americans were threatened by new diseases and the loss of tribal lands. Wars broke out, and during the 1800s, the U.S. Army forced the few remaining tribes to live on government reservations. Today, many Native Americans are reviving old traditions and teaching others about tribal art, religions, and medicine.

NERVOUS SYSTEM

The nervous system consists of the brain and the nerves, the bundles of fiber that connect the brain to the different parts of the body. It controls functions, such as breathing and the beating of the heart, which the body carries out automatically. It also enables the body to respond to outside events. A two-lane highway flows along the nerves. Some, known as sensory nerves, carry signals to the brain telling it about sensations such as heat, cold, and pain. Others, known as motor nerves, carry instructions from the brain to the body telling it how to react. If you touch something hot, for example, the sensory nerves carry pain signals to the brain, and the motor nerves carry back the instructions to jerk your hand away.

NEST

Many animals build nests for their young. Usually they are well hidden and out of reach of enemies. Some are simple; just scrapes in the ground or untidy piles of twigs. But many are elaborately built of mud, grass, moss, feathers, and wax. Birds, fish, insects, reptiles, and mammals build nests.

Nest: Weaver birds build their nests with the entrance facing downward to deter predators.

NETHERLANDS, BELGIUM, AND LUXEMBOURG

These three countries form the area of Europe known as the Low Countries. In 1948 they forged an economic union known as Benelux, and in 1957 they were founder members of the European Union.

The Netherlands is largely flat and much of it lies below sea level. It is well-known for its dikes and canals. Dairy farming, greenhouse vegetables, and horticulture are very important, but other industries are growing rapidly. The Dutch have a long and successful seafaring history and Rotterdam is the busiest port in Europe.

Belgium's population is divided into the Dutch-speaking Flemings in the north and the French-speaking Walloons in the south. Its capital, Brussels, is home to the European Parliament. Belgium is heavily industrialized and steel manufacturing is its most important industry.

Luxembourg is one of the smallest countries in Europe. It is an international center of banking and finance.

NEWTON, ISAAC (1642–1727)

Newton was one of the greatest scientists and mathematicians the world has known. He was the first person to explain the force of gravity, which holds the universe together. Newton carried out many experiments with light and split up light into a spectrum, or band of color. He built the first reflecting telescope and he invented calculus.

See also COLOR; GRAVITY; LIGHT; TELESCOPE.

NEW ZEALAND

Two long and narrow islands, the North Island and South Island, and a few smaller islands make up the country of New Zealand. It lies in the south Pacific Ocean.

New Zealand has mountains, volcanoes, hot springs, fast-flowing rivers, and glaciers. Most of the towns and cities are on the coast.

The grasslands are ideal for sheep and cattle farming. New Zealand is famous for its butter, cheese, and meat, and for fruit.

The native Maoris settled in New Zealand around 1,000 years ago. Although the Dutch explorer Abel Tasman discovered and named New Zealand in 1642, the country was mainly settled by people from Britain.

See also PAGE 63.

NIGERIA

Nigeria is named after the Niger River, which flows through the country to the Atlantic Ocean. Its landscape ranges from swampy plains and rain forests to grasslands and rock. It is one of the world's major oil producers, exports large quantities of cacao, peanuts, and

Nobel Prize: Alfred Nobel (1833–1896) left much of the fortune he had made from dynamite to fund six Nobel prizes.

palm oil, and has a growing tin- and coal-mining industry.

Nigeria's 111 million people are from a great number of different ethnic groups and speak many languages. Nigeria was a British colony from 1914 to 1960. Recent decades have been dominated by military rule, although there have been attempts at democracy.

NOBEL PRIZE

Every year six Nobel prizes may be awarded, for outstanding work in chemistry, physics, medicine, literature, economics, and the cause of peace. Two or three people may share a prize, and the winners may come from any part of the world. To win a Nobel prize is a very great honor. The money for the prizes was given by Alfred Nobel, a Swedish chemist, who invented dynamite.

NOMADS

Nomads are groups of people who wander from place to place with their animals and possessions. They do not build permanent houses. Some nomads keep flocks and herds, and move to find fresh grazing land for their animals.

NORTH AMERICA

This is the third largest of the Earth's continents. It stretches from the cold wastes of Alaska in the north to the hot deserts of Mexico and the tropical forests of Central America in the south. Canada and the United States cover most of North America.

Down the western side of North America run the rugged Rocky Mountains. In the center of the continent are wide grasslands called prairies. The Canadian Shield, a wild region of lakes and forests in northern Canada, has valuable minerals, such as coal and oil. In the south of the continent are coastal plains that are swampy in places. The longest river in North America is the Mississippi. The Great Lakes are the largest freshwater lakes in the world.

Crops grown in North America include wheat, fruit, vegetables, and cotton. Canada and the United States are great industrial countries, with plentiful raw materials.

North America is a continent of great contrasts. It has some of the world's largest cities, such as New York and Mexico City. But there are huge areas with hardly any people at all. The United States is one of the richest countries in the world, but in Central America the countries are small and poor.

The first people in North America came from Asia. They were the ancestors of the Native Americans, and the Inuit (or Eskimos). Europeans came much later, along with people from all over the world.

See also PAGES 62–63.

NUCLEAR ENERGY

Under certain conditions atoms of uranium can be made to split. When they do so, large amounts of energy are released as heat and light. The splitting of the atom, or rather of its nucleus, is called nuclear fission.

Scientists can now control the fission of uranium and use the energy it releases to produce nuclear power. In furnaces, called reactors, great heat is produced when the nucleus of the atom splits. This heat is used to drive turbines and generate electricity. Nuclear power is also used to drive some ships.

In atomic bombs, the nuclear reaction is uncontrolled and all the energy is released, causing devastation over a huge area.

NUT

Some trees bear fruit called nuts. Inside the tough shell of the nut is a seed. Ripe nuts fall to earth in the fall. The seed sends a new shoot pushing through the shell, and a new tree begins its life.

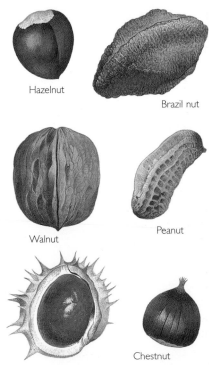

Hazelnut

Brazil nut

Walnut

Peanut

Horse chestnut

Chestnut

Nut: The hard shell of the nut protects the seed inside it.

OASIS

An oasis is a fertile area in a desert. Sometimes water comes to the surface naturally. Sometimes wells are sunk to tap it. Some oases cover many square miles and may support a city. Others have only a few huts.

OCEAN

Arorund 70 percent of the Earth's surface is covered by water. The large areas of salty water that separate the continents from each other are called oceans.

There are five oceans. The biggest and deepest is the Pacific Ocean, which separates the Americas and Asia. Next come the Atlantic Ocean and the Indian Ocean. The Antarctic and Arctic oceans surround the poles.

Around most coasts a shelf of land runs out under the sea. This is the continental shelf. It lies up to 600 feet deep, and may stretch for hundreds of miles. Beyond the continental shelf, the ocean floor drops away steeply. It flattens out again at a depth of around 12,000 feet. The bottom of the ocean is called the abyss. It is a flat plain, crossed by ridges, high

mountains, and deep trenches.

Life abounds in the oceans. Today, sea creatures range in size from enormous whales to tiny drifting animals, too small to be seen without a microscope. There are many marine plants, including huge seaweeds.

The oceans are never still. The rise and fall of the tides, which takes place approximately every 12 hours, is caused by the gravitational pull of the Earth and the Moon. The surface of the water is moved by waves, caused by the wind.

See also TIDES; WIND.

OCTOPUS AND SQUID

The octopus and squid are soft-bodied mollusks that live in the sea. Octopus means "eight feet," though we usually call its tentacles "arms." A squid has ten tentacles. Suckers on the tentacles

Octopus: *The octopus moves by jet propulsion, like the squid, but can also crawl slowly on its eight arms.*

seize and hold prey, which the animals eat with a sharp, "beak" in the center of their bodies. If danger threatens, an octopus can squirt an inky liquid that forms a cloud in the water, behind which the octopus can escape. A giant squid can be 33 feet long, including tentacles.

OIL

Oil is a greasy substance that does not mix with water. There are three kinds of oil: mineral, fatty, and "essential."

Mineral oil is distilled from petroleum. It comes from the Earth's crust and is used for fuels and lubricants.

Oil: *Undersea oil deposits can be reached from a platform perched on long legs. Engineers bore down through the rock to reach the oil.*

Fatty oils come from both animals and vegetables. Linseed oil, lard, butter, and margarine are fatty oils.

Essential oils give scents and flavors to flowers and fruits. Lemon oil from lemon rind, and cinnamon from bark, are types of essential oils.

OLYMPIC GAMES

Between 776 B.C. and A.D. 393, the ancient Greeks held athletic contests on the plain of Olympia every four years in honor of the god Zeus. The idea was taken up again in 1896, when the first modern Olympics were held at Athens. The Games are now held once every four years, each time in a different country, and many nations take part in the different sports. The winners receive gold, silver, and bronze medals. The most recent Olympic Games were held in 1996 in Atlanta, Georgia.

OPERA

An opera is a play in which the actors sing the words of the story. The first operas were written in Italy in the 1600s. The actors recited the story to music. Later, complete songs called arias were added. Many operas tell sad stories, but some are cheerful and have happy endings. Famous composers of operas include Monteverdi, Verdi, Mozart, Puccini, and Wagner.

ORCHESTRA

The word "orchestra" is used to describe any group of musicians, large or small, which plays together under a conductor. There are various types: large symphony orchestras of around a hundred musicians, small chamber orchestras, orchestras with stringed instruments only, and theater orchestras for musicals, ballets, and opera.

The conductor directs and interprets the music, giving it its life and character. He or she indicates the speed, rhythm, expression, and loudness of the music.

Orchestra: A typical orchestra is made up of around 20 different kinds of instrument, which are divided into four main sections— strings, woodwind, brass, and percussion.

OTTER

Otters belong to the weasel family. They are excellent swimmers. They paddle through

Percussion

Brass

Woodwind

Strings

the water with their webbed toes and use their strong tails as rudders. Their thick fur keeps out the wet and cold. The river otter eats mostly fish and frogs. Its home is a hole in the riverbank called a holt. The sea otter is larger and rarely comes on land.

Ottoman Empire

With its center in present-day Turkey, the Ottoman Empire was once huge, including a large part of southeastern Europe and most of the Middle East and North Africa. Its rulers, known as sultans, were Muslims—followers of the Islamic faith.

The first Ottoman ruler was Osman I (1258–c.1326). The greatest was Suleiman the Magnificent (c.1494–1566). During his reign the Ottoman Empire reached the peak of its power, threatening to spread into Western Europe. It then declined slowly until it finally fell apart after World War I. The last sultan, Muhammad VI, gave up his throne in 1922.

Owl

Owls are birds of prey. Their large eyes see well in the dark and they fly noiselessly on their broad wings. Hunting at night, they swoop down on small animals,

Owl: *The barn owl favors heaths, woods, fields, and hedges.*

such as mice and voles, and carry them off in their strong claws. The owl rips flesh with its hooked beak but it cannot digest fur, skin, and bones. It spits them out in the form of a pellet.

Oxygen

Oxygen, a colorless, odorless gas, is the most common element on Earth. It combines easily with minerals and other substances. Oxygen is found in air, water, and many different rocks.

All living things need oxygen. Animals need extra oxygen to move around, and fire needs oxygen in order to burn.

P

PACIFIC OCEAN

The Pacific Ocean is the largest
and the deepest of all the world's
oceans. Its deepest part could
cover the world's highest
mountain. The Pacific washes
the shores of western North
and South America, eastern Asia,
and Australia, and stretches
from the Arctic to Antarctica.

Thousands of islands in the
Pacific were formed from
volcanoes. Movements in the
Earth's crust around the fringes
of the Pacific often cause
earthquakes and sometimes
tidal waves.

Many of the tiny islands
sprinkled over the Pacific are
inhabited, including the islands
of Melanesia (meaning "black
islands"), Micronesia ("small
islands") and Polynesia
("many islands").

Some of the world's tiniest
nations are here, countries such
as Tuvalu and Kiribati. Tuvalu,
for example, is part of Polynesia.
It consists of nine coral islands.
Put together these islands
cover only 10 square miles,
yet they are spread out in a
chain that is around 370 miles
long. Only 9,000 people live
on them.

PAINTING

The oldest known paintings were
made by Stone Age people in
caves thousands of years ago.
Much later, people started to
decorate their homes and temples
with paintings. Egyptians, Greeks,
Romans, and Chinese painted
vases, pottery, and walls.

During the Middle Ages in
Europe, most paintings were done
for churches, so painters mainly
painted stories from the Bible.
Later, Italian painters began to
paint Bible characters who looked
like real people.

During the Renaissance, painters

FAMOUS PAINTERS

Giotto	Italian (c.1266–1337)
Jan van Eyck	Flemish (c.1387–1440)
Sandro Botticelli	Italian (c.1444–1510)
Leonardo da Vinci	Italian (1452–1519)
Albrecht Dürer	German (1471–1528)
Michelangelo	Italian (1475–1564)
Titian	Italian (1477–1576)
Raphael	Italian (1483–1520)
El Greco	Spanish (c.1541–1614)
Rubens	Flemish (1577–1640)
Velázquez	Spanish (c.1599–1666)
Rembrandt van Rijn	Dutch (1606–1669)
Goya	Spanish (1746–1828)
J. M. W. Turner	English (1775–1851)
Edouard Manet	French (1832–1883)
Paul Cézanne	French (1839–1906)
Henri Rousseau	French (1844–1910)
Vincent van Gogh	Dutch (1853–1890)
Vassily Kandinsky	Russian (1866–1944)
Henri Matisse	French (1869–1954)
Pablo Picasso	Spanish (1881–1973)
Jackson Pollock	U.S.A. (1912–1956)

Greek and Roman legends as their subjects. They also painted portraits of people from life, and realistic scenes from nature. During the 1700s, many painters worked for fashionable society. They painted people in family groups, often against a background of a garden or a fine house.

Artists have always experimented with new ideas. Impressionist painters, for instance, loved to paint light and shadow, and ignored the details, which could be captured perfectly in a photograph. By the early 1900s, some were making pictures as designs and shapes, rather than as copies of objects. This is called abstract painting.

See also LEONARDO DA VINCI; MICHELANGELO; PICASSO.

PANDA

One of the world's rarest animals is the giant panda. It looks like a furry black and white bear.

Pandas live in bamboo forests in the mountains of China. They eat mostly bamboo shoots and leaves. Pandas do not breed easily in captivity, so few have been seen in zoos outside China.

PAPER

The word paper comes from "papyrus," the reed the Egyptians used to make paper. The type of paper we use today was invented by the Chinese around A.D. 105. It was made of mulberry bark. Small pieces of bark were soaked to separate the fibers, then dried into flat sheets.

With the invention of the printing press in the 1400s, the demand for paper grew. In 1799,

Paper: Paper is made by crushing or chemically treating logs to make wood pulp, which is made into a thin slurry with water. The slurry passes on to a loop of wire mesh and, as the water is sucked out, the wood fibers form a web of paper. The web is squeezed between rollers, dried, and usually coated with substances to make it smooth and white.

Log | Chipper | Washing unit | Screen | Wire

Debarked log

Louis Robert invented a machine to produce a continuous reel of paper. Today, most paper is made on machines from wood pulp obtained from tree fibers.

PARASITE

A parasite lives in or on a larger living thing and feeds on it. It is an uninvited guest. The animal or plant on which it lives is called a host. Parasites often harm their hosts by taking too much food, or by causing diseases. Mistletoe, tapeworms, fleas, lice, and mosquitoes are examples of parasites.

PASTEUR, LOUIS (1822–1895)

Pasteur was a French scientist. He proved that bacteria and other germs cause diseases. Pasteur injected weakened germs into animals and people to keep them from catching the diseases that those germs usually caused.

He invented pasteurization: a method of heating milk and cooling it quickly to make it safe to drink. Pasteur also found out how tiny yeast cells turn sugar into alcohol.

PEARL HARBOR

Pearl Harbor in Hawaii was the site of the surprise Japanese air attack on the U.S. Pacific Fleet on December 7, 1941. In less than two hours, five battleships and 188 planes were destroyed. More than 2,000 Americans lay dead and 1,200 were wounded. The United States declared war on Japan as a result and entered World War II on the side of the Allies.

See also WORLD WAR II.

PENGUIN

Penguins are seabirds that live on coasts around Antarctica. Unable to fly, penguins use their wings as paddles and are excellent swimmers. They have a layer of thick fat to keep out the cold. Some kinds of penguins lay their eggs in rough nests on the rocks.

PERFUME

Perfume is a fragrant essence in which more than 100 natural aromatic (sweet-smelling or spicy) materials may be blended. The materials come from around 60,000 different flowers, leaves, fruits, seeds, woods, barks, resins, and roots.

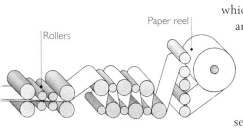

Paper reel

Rollers

PETER THE GREAT
(1672–1725)
As king, or czar, of Russia, Peter the Great turned his country into one of Europe's most powerful nations. One of his ambitions was to build Russian ports on the shores of the Baltic Sea and the Black Sea. These would give Russia better contact with Western Europe. In 1695–1696 he fought a war with Turkey and won a firm foothold on the Black Sea. He also wanted to modernize his country, and in 1697–1698 he toured western Europe to find out about the most up-to-date ways of doing things. Later he built a new Russian capital, St. Petersburg, on the Baltic coast. He fought a long war against Sweden, winning a great victory at the Battle of Poltava in 1709.

PHILIPPINES
The Philippines is a nation made up of over 7,000 islands in the western Pacific. It is a producer of chromite, nickel, and copper, as well as sugarcane, fruit, and Manila hemp. Governed first by Spain and then by the United States, it became independent in 1946. In 1986 its virtual dictator, Ferdinand Marcos, was ousted, and in democratic elections Corazón Aquino came to power. She was replaced in 1992 by Fidel Ramos.
    See also PAGE 62.

PHOTOGRAPHY
Photography was invented in 1839 by Louis Daguerre in France and William Fox Talbot in England.
    Today there are inexpensive

Photosynthesis: *Respiration is almost the reverse process of photosynthesis: carbon dioxide and water vapor are released from the leaves into the air.*

Water

Light energy

Carbon dioxide

Chlorophyll

Oxygen

PHOTOSYNTHESIS

Carbon dioxide

Water

RESPIRATION

cameras that work automatically, as well as the complex equipment, processes, and techniques used by television and movies, and in medical and scientific research.

See also CAMERA.

PHOTOSYNTHESIS

This is the process by which plants make food. Water from the soil and carbon dioxide gas from the air are combined to form sugars. This process can take place only in living plant cells that contain the green coloring matter, chlorophyll. The energy comes from sunlight.

Picasso: *Pablo Picasso was one of the most influential figures in 20th-century art.*

PHYSICS

Physics is the branch of science practiced by physicists. They study matter and energy and how they relate to one another. This includes subjects such as electricity, magnetism, and mechanics. An important branch of modern physics is the study of the atom and the minute particles that make it up.

PICASSO, PABLO (1881–1973)

Picasso was a Spanish artist who greatly influenced art in the 1900s. His painting changed from a realistic style to abstract styles like cubism, which uses shapes such as cubes, triangles, and geometrical shapes.

PIG

The pig is a very useful, intelligent animal. We eat its meat as pork, sausages, bacon, and ham, its skin can be made into leather, and its bristles go into brushes. Male pigs are called boars; and females, sows. Pigs are unjustly accused of being dirty. They wallow in mud to keep themselves clean as well as cool.

PIRATE

Until around 150 years ago, sea voyagers had more to fear than sudden storms. They faced the added danger of pirates. These fierce bands of sea robbers sailed the seas in fast, well-armed ships. When they saw a merchant ship,

173

they chased and captured it. They stole its cargo and robbed the passengers of their belongings.

Some pirates became rich. Most were caught and hanged. By the 1800s, ships could sail most seas without fear of pirates.

PIZARRO, FRANCISCO (c.1475–1541)

Pizarro became one of the most famous of the conquistadores, the men who conquered large parts of the Americas for Spain. In 1530, he landed with 180 followers on the coast of Peru. Two years later, he and his tiny army had captured the ruler of the vast Inca Empire. In 1533, they captured the Inca capital, Cuzco, high in the Andes Mountains. They had done all this using clever trickery. They also had guns and horses, which gave them an advantage over the Incas, who had neither.

PLANET

See SOLAR SYSTEM.

PLANKTON

This is the drifting life of the sea. It is made up of tiny and microscopic plants, and animals that float at or near the surface. Every sea animal depends in some way on plankton, because small fish feed on it and are eaten in turn by larger fish.

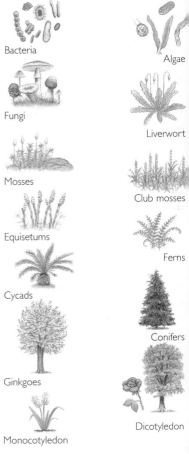

Bacteria

Algae

Fungi

Liverwort

Mosses

Club mosses

Equisetums

Ferns

Cycads

Conifers

Ginkgoes

Monocotyledon

Dicotyledon

Plant: Botanists have classed plants into groups, mainly by the way they are built and the way they reproduce.

PLANT

There are more than 335,000 kinds of plant. Most plants are green. The green color is caused by a substance called chlorophyll. This is used by the plant to make its food. The way it does this is called photosynthesis.

The plant kingdom includes several groups. The simplest plants are algae. Some algae are simply a single cell, which reproduces itself by splitting in two. Others, such as seaweeds, are much bigger.

Fungi are plants that have no chlorophyll, so they are not green and cannot make their own food. Instead, they feed on rotting or dead matter.

Mosses and liverworts are another group. They live on land. But, like fungi, they have no real roots, and no flowers. Ferns are more advanced. They have stems, leaves, and roots, but they cannot make flowers and seeds.

There are two kinds of flowering plants. Monocotyledons, such as lilies, daffodils, and grasses, have long, straight leaves. Dicotyledons, such as peas, roses, and broad-leaved trees, have broad leaves.

Seed-bearing plants produce male and female cells. The cells join to form a fertile seed, which grows into a new plant.

See also ALGAE; FERN; FLOWER; GRASS; LEAF; LICHEN; MOSS; MUSHROOM AND TOADSTOOL; PHOTOSYNTHESIS; SEED; TREE.

PLASTICS

Plastics are man-made materials that have a wide variety of uses. They can be made into furniture, car bodies, clothing, and crockery. There are many different kinds of plastics, all of which can be shaped easily. Many of them are shaped by blowing, squirting, or pressing into molds.

Important plastics include nylon, polyethylene, PVC, and polystyrene. All are made with chemicals obtained from oil. Some plastics are made from wood.

PLATO (c.428–347 B.C.)

Plato was one of the world's most important thinkers. He came from the ancient Greek city of Athens and was a pupil and friend of Socrates. In around 386 B.C., he set up a school at Athens called the Academy. In his most famous book, *The Republic*, he described a system for educating a "philosopher king," his idea of the perfect ruler.

PLATYPUS

The strange duck-billed platypus is a mammal that lays eggs. It lives in Australia. It has webbed feet, a tail like a beaver, thick fur, and a ducklike bill. The platypus lives in a burrow in a riverbank, and feeds underwater on insects, worms, and shellfish.

PLAY

Plays were first performed in ancient Greece. Some were tragedies: plays that tell a serious story and often have sad endings. Others were comedies: plays with happy endings.

In the Middle Ages people performed miracle and mystery plays—stories from the Bible—or morality plays, in which the hero (main character) met a number of good and bad characters.

Some of the first indoor theaters were built in England in the 1500s. Companies of actors performed the plays of Shakespeare, Marlowe, and Jonson. There was not much scenery, and actors wore the clothes of their own day. Boys took women's parts, as women were not allowed to act.

Since the 1700s and 1800s plays have become closer to real life. They are written in simple, everyday language, and the plots (stories) are usually about the lives of ordinary people.

POETRY

The oldest stories we know were first told as poetry. In a poem the words are often arranged to a musical beat or rhythm. Poetry which is written in a meter, or rhythm, is known as verse. But the rhythm does not have to be regular all the time. This would be dull. Blank verse has a rhythm, but it does not rhyme. Shakespeare used blank verse in his plays. Modern poets often

FAMOUS PLAYWRIGHTS

Aeschylus	Greek (c.525–456 B.C.)
Sophocles	Greek (496–406 B.C.)
Euripides	Greek (480–406 B.C.)
Aristophanes	Greek (c.450–406 B.C.)
William Shakespeare	English (1564–1616)
Ben Jonson	English (1572–1637)
Jean Baptiste Racine	French (1639–1699)
Richard Brinsley Sheridan	Irish (1751–1816)
Henrik Ibsen	Norwegian (1828–1906)
Oscar Wilde	Irish (1854–1900)
George Bernard Shaw	Irish (1856–1950)
Anton Chekhov	Russian (1860–1904)
Jean Cocteau	French (1889–1963)
Bertolt Brecht	German (1898–1956)
Samuel Beckett	Irish (1906–1990)
Tennessee Williams	American (1911–1983)
Neil Simon	American (born 1927)
Harold Pinter	English (born 1930)

prefer free verse, which does not rhyme or have a strict rhythm.

There are different styles and forms of poetry. Story poems with short verses and, often, with exciting stories are called ballads. Long story-poems are called epics.

The greatest of the ancient epic poems, full of the deeds of brave heroes, are the *Iliad* and *Odyssey* written by Homer, a Greek, and the *Aeneid* of the Roman poet Virgil.

Expressions of poets' feelings are called lyrics. They include such forms as the song, sonnet, ode, elegy, and pastoral. Plays are sometimes written in poetry and these are called dramatic poems.

POISON

A poison is a substance that attacks the body, and can cause sickness or death. Some poisons are dangerous when swallowed. Others damage the lungs, the skin, and the nervous system. Chemicals, drugs, gases, acids, and spoiled food can all be poisonous. Some medicines are poisonous if used incorrectly: always to follow the directions carefully.

POLLUTION

Pollution is the contamination of soil, water, or the atmosphere by harmful substances. Chemicals used to kill insects and weeds can build up and damage the soil. Sewage, waste from factories, and oil from tankers pollute rivers and oceans. Smoke from chimneys and fumes from cars pollute the air.

Pollution can threaten our health, and even make it impossible for plants and animals to live. People are trying to find ways to prevent pollution.

POPE

The Pope is the head of the Roman Catholic Church and bishop of Rome. St. Peter was the first bishop of Rome. The Pope lives in the Vatican, a tiny independent state in Rome. His chief advisers are the cardinals. They elect a new pope.

Pollution: The gases that produce acid rain are released by power stations, factories, and transport.

Factory fumes | Acid drains into river | Acid rain

PORCUPINE

Porcupines are rodents. They live in forests and eat twigs, leaves, and fruit. The porcupines of Africa and Asia live on the ground, but North and South American porcupines are good climbers.

PORTUGAL

See SPAIN AND PORTUGAL.

POST OFFICE

In early times, messages were carried by runners or by riders on horseback. In the United States, mail used to be delivered by pony express, stagecoach, and train. The world's first regular airmail service started in the United States in 1918. Today, most U.S. mail is airmail. The United States now has the largest postal system in the world, and handles billions of pieces of mail each year.

See also STAMP.

POTATO

Potatoes are important food plants. The part you eat is a tuber, a swollen underground stem, in which the plant stores food. New plants grow from the "eyes" in the starchy tubers.

The potato plant grows wild in the Andes of South America. Explorers brought potatoes to Europe in the 1500s.

Porcupine: Sharp quills, or spines, cover the body of the North American porcupine.

PRAIRIE

Prairies are large areas of flat or rolling grasslands, found particularly in central North America. Once they were home to prairie grasses and animals such as bison and wolves, but now their fertile soil is farmed for corn and wheat, or they are grazed by cattle. Only small, protected areas of native prairie are now left.

PREHISTORIC ANIMAL

The first animals appeared in the sea more than 700 million years ago. They may have been shaped like tiny blobs of jelly. Later, some kinds developed protective shells.

One common group, trilobites, looked like pill bugs. All of these early animals were invertebrates.

The first vertebrate animals (animals with backbones) were the fish, which appeared around 450 million years ago. At this time, the land was almost empty. There were plants and insectlike creatures, but no vertebrates. Around 400 million years ago, some fish crawled out of the water onto the land. They slowly developed legs instead of fins, and lungs with which they could breathe. They were the first amphibians.

Then came the reptiles. They adapted to different ways of life. Many were plant eaters, but some were hunters, preying on other reptiles. Around 200 million years ago dinosaurs appeared. For millions of years dinosaurs ruled the Earth. The word dinosaur means "terrible lizard." Some dinosaurs were very small, but others were huge, and were the largest land animals that have ever lived. The last dinosaurs died out around 65 million years ago, but we know something of what they looked like from their fossil remains.

There were plant-eating and meat-eating dinosaurs. Among the plant eaters were the biggest dinosaurs, such as *Brachiosaurus* and *Diplodocus*. They walked on four thick legs, and had long necks and tails. Some giant dinosaurs were nearly 100 feet long. Others weighed 80 tons.

Meat-eating dinosaurs were smaller and most of them ran on their hind legs. The largest and fiercest was *Tyrannosaurus*, the "tyrant lizard." It stood 18 feet high and weighed 7 tons. It had huge, sharp claws and long, sharp teeth.

Prehistoric Animal: *This parade of prehistoric animals includes the tallest, the longest, the fiercest, and the most stupid dinosaur.*

Despite their size, dinosaurs had tiny brains. Scientists are not sure why they became extinct. Perhaps the climate became cooler, and the vegetation changed, so that the dinosaurs could not keep warm or get enough food.

The first true birds may have evolved from dinosaurs which lived in trees, and could just manage to glide from branch to branch.

The first mammals were small, insect-eating animals. When the dinosaurs died out, the little mammals took over and many different kinds developed. Many became extinct during the Ice Ages, however, when they were killed by a new mammal—man the hunter.

See also EVOLUTION; FOSSIL; ICE AGE; MAMMOTH.

PREHISTORIC PEOPLE

Prehistoric people lived before the beginning of written history. The first humans appeared some 200,000 years ago. The first written records appeared in the Middle East around 3300 B.C., but not on some South Pacific islands until around 200 years ago.

Prehistoric people hunted and fished, made tools, implements and pottery, farmed, and made dwellings. We know about them through the study of archaeology. Archaeologists investigate the places where they lived and study the bones and objects that they find there.

PRESIDENT

The United States, France, Italy, and many other countries all have a president. He or she is the head of state. In the United States, the president is also head of government.

PRIME MINISTER

A prime minister is a head of government. The prime minister usually leads the political party that has been voted the most seats in parliament. He or she chooses people called ministers to help run the government.

Prehistoric People: Homo erectus, *an early type of man, searches for roots, shoots, and grubs in the soil.*

PRINTING

Before the 1400s, the usual way to produce books was to copy them by hand, so they were rare and expensive. Then, around 1450, Johannes Gutenberg made copies of the Bible on a printing press.

Gutenberg's method of printing was to build up his words from separate pieces of type, ink the type, then press paper against it. Printing by inking metal type (called letterpress) is still used, but many books are now printed by a photographic process (called lithography). The words are made up on a piece of film, and flat printing plates are made from the film. The plates are treated so that they pick up the ink only where the words are.

PROTEIN

Proteins are the building blocks of life. They are substances in foods that build body tissue and repair cells. They contain carbon, hydrogen, oxygen, and nitrogen. Proteins also provide heat and energy. Most of our proteins come from meat, fish, and cheese. Plants such as peanuts, beans, and peas also contain quantities of protein.

PYRAMID

The ancient Egyptians buried their pharaohs (kings) in tombs called pyramids. They had four triangular sides meeting at a pointed top.

Some are made of more than two million blocks of stone. Thousands of slaves dragged the huge stones slowly into place. Inside was a tomb where the mummy of the pharaoh was laid, surrounded by treasure. The best-known pyramids are a group of three built at Giza around 2680–2565 B.C.

PYTHAGORAS (c.580–500 B.C.)

Pythagoras was an ancient Greek astronomer, mathematician, and philosopher. He was one of the first to teach that the Earth and the other planets revolved around the sun. Perhaps his best-known contribution to geometry is the Pythagorean theorem.

Pythagoras: Pythagoras' theorem states that the square of the hypotenuse of a right-angled triangle is equal to the sum of the squares of the other two sides.

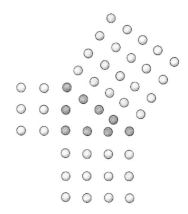

R

Rabbit and Hare

Rabbits are burrowing animals. They live in colonies called warrens. Rabbits breed rapidly.

Hares look like rabbits. But they are bigger, with longer ears and legs. Hares are swift runners. Unlike rabbits, they live alone in hollows called forms.

Raccoon

The raccoon has long gray fur, a short pointed nose, and a bushy tail ringed with black. Raccoons live in North America.

Radar

Radar stands for "radio detecting and ranging." It is a device that can "see" faraway objects by bouncing radio waves off them. The waves travel like echoes back to the radar. They are picked up by the radar antennae and show up as small dots of light on a screen. From the position of the dot, the location of the object can be figured out. Ships and planes rely on radar for safety.

Radio

Radio depends on radio waves. These invisible waves travel as fast as light waves. Radio works because radio waves can be made to carry signals that represent sound.

In a radio broadcasting studio, sounds go into a microphone, where they are changed to electrical signals. These signals are combined with a "carrier" wave, and transmitted by an antenna.

The antenna of a radio receiver picks up the carrier wave. Circuits in the receiver remove the carrier wave and leave only the electrical signals carrying the sound. These are fed to a loudspeaker, which gives out the same sounds that went into the studio microphone.

Radar: Radar can detect the direction, speed, and distance of an aircraft by bouncing radio waves off it.

Reflected waves

Transmitted waves

Radar screen

Radioactivity

The atoms of most chemical elements do not change. But the atoms of some elements are unstable and emit (give out) atomic particles or radiation. We call this process radioactivity. Uranium and radium are radioactive elements.

See also ATOM; NUCLEAR ENERGY.

Alpha particle
Beta particle
Gamma ray

Paper Aluminum Steel

RAILROAD

The first public railroad to use steam locomotives was the Stockton and Darlington line in the north of England. It was opened in 1825. George Stephenson, an engineer, built the ten-mile track and its first engine, which was called *Locomotion.*

Steam locomotives, belching smoke, hauled passenger trains and freight cars for more than 100 years. But there are few left today. They have been replaced by diesel and electric locomotives, which are cleaner, quieter, and cheaper to run.

Until the beginning of this century the railroads had no rivals. Then the automobile and the airplane were invented. Railroads were used less and less, and many lines closed. Now, new trains can travel twice as fast as automobiles.

RAIN AND HAIL

Rain comes from the water in seas, lakes, rivers, and soil. The Sun's heat turns some of this

Radioactivity: The three forms of radioactivity, alpha, beta, and gamma radiation, have different penetrating abilities.

water into water vapor which rises in the air. As the rising air cools, some of the water vapor "condenses" or turns back into water droplets, and becomes visible as clouds. As the air rises higher, more and more vapor turns back into water and the clouds grow bigger and darker. Finally, water droplets from the clouds fall to the ground as rain.

Sometimes the water droplets inside a thundercloud are carried so high and become so cold that they freeze into ice pellets. These may eventually fall to the ground as hailstones.

See also CLOUD.

RECORDING

Modern records are disks of plastic that "store" sound in their grooves. Another way to record sound is on tape. Here, the sound is recorded in the form of a magnetic pattern. Cassettes carry reels of tape that can be played back on a home or car cassette player.

Television programs can now be recorded on disk and tape. The sound track in movies is often recorded as an image on the film.

See also VIDEOTAPE.

RED CROSS

The Red Cross organization helps the victims of wars and disasters. In 1859, the armies of France and Austria fought a terrible battle in Italy. A Swiss traveler, Jean Henri Dunant, saw thousands of wounded soldiers who had been abandoned. He tried to help them, and wrote a book describing what he had seen. As a result, the Red Cross was formed in Geneva, Switzerland (a country that never takes part in war). The organization's flag is a red cross on a white background.

REFORMATION

This movement in the 1500s ended the religious unity of western Europe and led to the establishment of the various Protestant Churches.

Until 1500, all Christians were Roman Catholics, with the Pope as their spiritual head. Martin Luther,

a German monk, disagreed with many of its teachings and protested in 1517. Many people agreed with him and a split developed. But not all Protestants believed the same things, so the movement itself split into many types of Protestantism.

REFRIGERATION

Food lasts longer when it is kept cool in a refrigerator. Cooling slows down the processes that make food

Red Cross: *This French Renault Red Cross ambulance dates from World War I.*

spoil. Freezers keep food fresh for longer periods.

Refrigerators are worked by electricity or gas. They have a pump that turns a vapor into liquid. The liquid is turned into vapor again inside the freezing compartment. As it does so, it absorbs heat from the food. In another part of the refrigerator, the vapor is changed back into a liquid and recirculated.

REFUGEE

People who are forced to flee from their homes and take refuge in another area or country are called refugees. Refugees are mainly escaping from invasion or war, but some flee to avoid violence or poverty in their own country. Some eventually return home; others settle in the new place.

RELIGION

A religion is a belief, a way of living, or both. It may mean belief in a god or gods with powers greater than our own, and in another life after this one. It may involve prayer and worship.

All the world's great religions began in Asia. The oldest religion to teach that there is only one god is Judaism, the religion of the Jews.

The followers of Islam are called Muslims. Muslims believe in Allah, the one god. Their holy book is called the Koran.

Hinduism is the main religion of India. Hindus believe people's souls are reborn many times.

Buddhism is another important Eastern religion. Its founder, Buddha ("The Enlightened One"), taught people how to escape from suffering and find peace.

People who follow the teachings of Jesus Christ are Christians.

Other important world religions are Confucianism, Taoism, Shintoism, and Sikhism.

See also BIBLE; BUDDHA AND BUDDHISM; HINDUISM; JESUS CHRIST; KORAN; MAGIC; MUHAMMAD.

REMBRANDT VAN RIJN (1606–1669)

Rembrandt was a Dutch artist who has become one of the most famous painters in the world. He was a master in the use of light, color, and mood.

RENAISSANCE

In the 1300s, a rebirth of learning began in Europe. Scholars rediscovered and studied the

Renaissance: The Tempietto in Rome marked a return in European architecture to the classical lines used by the ancient Greeks.

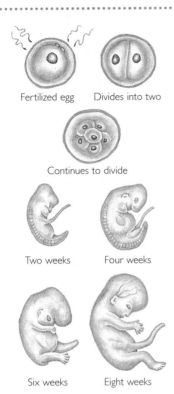

Fertilized egg   Divides into two

Continues to divide

Two weeks   Four weeks

Six weeks   Eight weeks

Reproduction: Once a human egg has been fertilized, it starts to divide to make countless new cells.

ancient writings of Greece and Rome. Artists such as Leonardo da Vinci and Michelangelo recaptured the beauty of "classical" Greek architecture and sculpture. Scientists such as Copernicus and Galileo questioned the old ideas about the universe. "Humanist" thinkers taught that human beings were not just weak creatures ruled by God.

REPRODUCTION

All animals and plants can reproduce. Simple animals and plants can reproduce on their own. They either divide into two (like the amoeba) or make special cells that grow into new plants (like fungi).

More advanced forms of life reproduce sexually by producing special sex cells. When a male cell joins with and fertilizes a female cell, this grows into a new individual. In flowering plants a male sex cell stored in a pollen grain joins a female sex cell in the carpel. In animals, the male cells are called sperm, and the female cells, eggs.

See also ANIMAL; CELL; FLOWER; GENETICS; HUMAN BODY.

REPTILE

Reptiles are cold-blooded animals —their body temperature is the same as the temperature of their surroundings. Because of this, reptiles cannot live in very cold lands. In places where there are cold winters, they hibernate.

Reptiles have tough, scaly skins and most lay leathery-shelled eggs. Baby reptiles hatch fully developed and are not cared for by their parents.

There are four main groups of reptiles: alligators and crocodiles, snakes and lizards, tortoises and turtles, and the very rare tuatara.

Most eat insects and small animals, but some eat plants.

See also CROCODILE AND ALLIGATOR; LIZARD; SNAKE; TURTLE AND TORTOISE.

RESPIRATION
See PHOTOSYNTHESIS.

REVOLUTION
The word revolution means "turn around" or "complete change." If a country has a revolution, its government and laws are overthrown, often by war and bloodshed.

The most famous revolutions in history happened in the United States, France, and Russia. In 1776, the American colonies broke away from Britain and became an independent republic. The French Revolution, in 1789, overthrew the king and the nobles who ruled France. In 1917, the rule of the Russian Czar was ended, and the world's first communist government was established.

RHINOCEROS
The rhinoceros is the second-largest land animal, after the elephant. The black rhinoceros and the white rhinoceros live on the African plains. Actually, both are gray. The rhinoceroses of India, Java, and Sumatra live in dense forests. Rhinoceroses eat grass, shoots, and twigs.

RICE
Rice is a member of the grass family. Its grains are one of the most important cereals grown. It is a staple food for many people in Asia, though it is grown and eaten in many other parts of the world. Rice is planted in flooded fields called paddies. The young shoots are grown in 3 to 4 inches of water. Rice has long, narrow leaves and clusters of flowers that turn into the rice grains.

RIVER
Rivers begin their lives as small streams in hills or mountains. Some begin as trickles of water from melting glaciers. Others bubble up through the ground as springs. Gravity makes water flow downhill. At first the river

Rhinoceros: Oxpeckers keep the rhinoceros's skin clean by eating the ticks and insects that settle there.

River: *As the river moves farther away from its source, its valley becomes shallower and smoother.*

rushes along, fed by rain and melting snow. When it reaches flatter country, the river flows more slowly. Other streams, called tributaries, may join it.

Finally, the river flows into the sea, sometimes through a fan-shaped network of channels known as a delta. The fresh water of many a river meets the salt water of the sea in a river mouth, or estuary.

See also WATER.

ROAD

Roads are made in layers. Tarmac roads have layers of tar and stones on top of well-rammed soil. Concrete roads are made of layers of concrete.

John McAdam was a pioneer road maker in the 1800s, and Italians built the first motorway in the 1920s. Two thousand years before, their ancestors, the Romans, were building fine roads throughout Europe, North Africa, and the Middle East.

ROBOT

Robots are programmable machines with arms that can move in several directions. Robots can be instructed to carry out different tasks. The instructions or programs are stored in the robot's computer brain.

Most robots work in industry and do jobs such as paint spraying, welding, and heavy lifting and loading. Some robots work in places that are dangerous for humans, such as nuclear power stations and outer space.

See also COMPUTER.

ROCK

The inside of the Earth is a hot, molten mass. But the outer skin, or crust, is made of solid rock. All rocks belong to three groups: the igneous, the sedimentary, and the metamorphic. All igneous rocks were once molten (melted) and came from deep in the Earth. Sedimentary rocks are formed of layers of materials such as sand and clay, which have been cemented together under pressure. Metamorphic rocks have been changed from their original form to another by heat and pressure.

ROCKET

A rocket is a kind of engine. It works by shooting out a stream of gases backward. As the gases go backward, the rocket goes forward. The rocket works much like a jet engine. Both burn fuel to make hot gases, which shoot out in a stream. But the rocket carries its own oxygen to burn the fuel. The jet engine gets its oxygen from the air.

See also JET ENGINE.

RODENT

Rodents are mammals that have chisel-like front teeth that are specially adapted for gnawing. There are more than 6,000 species of rodent. Beavers, squirrels, gerbils, hamsters, and porcupines are all rodents.

They are found everywhere. Some are good swimmers, such as beavers with their webbed feet and paddlelike tails. Others, such as most squirrels, live in trees. Guinea pigs were originally mountain-dwellers— they were tamed long

ago by the people of the Andes in South America and raised for their meat.

Rats often live in cities, towns, and other places where humans live. They may eat and damage our food, and also spread disease. The smallest rodent is the mouse. The largest is the capybara, which is the shape and size of a pig.

Rodents have many enemies. They are preyed on by hawks, owls, snakes, foxes, and other animals.

Rocket: *The rocket* Saturn *launched* Apollo 11 *to the Moon on July 16, 1969.*

ROME, ANCIENT

According to legend, Rome was founded by twin brothers named Romulus and Remus. At first the Romans were ruled by foreign kings. But in 509 B.C., the people set up a republic and elected their own rulers. They fought against their neighbors and built a powerful army. In 217 B.C., the first emperor took power.

Without their army, the Romans would never have conquered and ruled their empire, which stretched from Britain to the Middle East.

The capital of the empire was originally the city of Rome, built on seven hills. In A.D. 395, the empire was divided into two. One half was ruled from Rome, the other from Byzantium (Constantinople).

Rome was no longer strong. Its government was dishonest, and the army could no longer fight off the barbarian raids. Around A.D. 476, the western empire fell, and Rome was destroyed. In the east, the Byzantine Empire lasted until 1453, when Constantinople was captured by the Turks.

See also BYZANTINE EMPIRE; CAESAR; HANNIBAL.

ROOSEVELT, FRANKLIN DELANO
(1882–1945)
Franklin D. Roosevelt became president of the United States in 1933 and remained in office until he died. He had wanted to keep the United States out of World War II. But once in the war he created an alliance with Britain and the U.S.S.R., and they eventually won.

RUBBER
Rubber trees grow in tropical countries such as Malaysia and Indonesia. To make rubber, cuts are made in the bark of the tree and a milky sap (latex) oozes out, which is treated with acid to produce crude rubber. Rubber is used to make the soles of shoes, tires, tubes, and many other things. A lot of the rubber used now is made by the plastics industry.

RUSSIA
With an area of 6,591,100 sq. mi., Russia is the largest of the ex-U.S.S.R. republics. A train journey from its western border to the Pacific coast takes more than a week. Russia's population is around 147 million and its capital is Moscow.

RUTHERFORD, ERNEST
(1871–1937)
Rutherford was a New Zealand-born British physicist. He was a pioneer of atomic science and his main research was in the field of radioactivity. Rutherford was the first to "split" the atom. He won the Nobel chemistry prize in 1908.

S

SAINT

A saint is a holy person whom Christians believe came close to being perfect. Some saints, such as St. Francis of Assisi, are remembered for their good lives. Others, such as St. Bernadette of Lourdes, are believed to have performed miracles of healing.

To become a saint a person must be canonized with the approval of the Roman Catholic Church. A commission is set up by the Church to carefully examine everything about the person's life.

SALT

Salts make up a class of chemicals. There are many different salts, but the one we know best is the salt we eat—common salt. It is made from the two elements sodium and chlorine. Our bodies need salt. There is salt in blood, sweat, and in tears.

SATELLITE

A satellite is a small body in space that circles around a larger one. The Moon is the Earth's satellite. It circles the Earth once a month.

Satellite: Communications satellites pick up and transmit TV and telephone signals.

Most planets have satellites. We often call them moons.

The Earth now has many man-made satellites circling around it. The first artificial satellite, named *Sputnik I*, was launched by the Russians in 1957. To resist Earth's gravity, a satellite must speed around at 17,400 mph. Satellites can be very useful. Some help in weather forecasting. Some relay telephone and television signals all over the world.

SCANDINAVIA AND FINLAND

Scandinavia (Sweden, Norway, Denmark, and Iceland) and Finland, in northern Europe, are among the northernmost inhabited areas of the world. Northern Scandinavia—populated by the Sami (Lapps)—lies inside the Arctic Circle and has an Arctic climate, while the south is kept mild by the Gulf Stream, a warm ocean current.

The scenery is the legacy of the Ice Age, with ice caps, glaciers, mountains, lakes, and sea inlets called fjords. Iceland also has active volcanoes, including a new one, Surtsey, which emerged in 1963.

The area is rich in natural resources such as timber, iron ore, and offshore oil and gas from the North Sea. Fishing, shipbuilding, forestry, and farming are all important industries.

Sculpture: The art of making attractive models and statues is very ancient, as some of the earlier examples show.

c.5750 B.C.

c.2300 B.C.

C.A.D. 700

C.A.D. 1850

SCIENCE

The word "science" just means knowledge. In science, people try to find out about the world around them by observing things and carrying out experiments. Scientists try to classify new facts, and fit them in with what they know already.

Chemistry, physics, and biology are the main branches of science. Chemistry studies the way matter is arranged. Physics looks at the properties of matter and energy, and biology studies living things.

See also CHEMISTRY; ZOOLOGY.

SCOTT, ROBERT (1868–1912)

Robert Falcon Scott was a British naval commander and explorer. In 1911, he led an expedition to the South Pole, but reached it on January 18, 1912, to find that the Norwegian Roald Amundsen had arrived there first. Scott and the other members of his expedition died on the return journey.

SCULPTURE

Making models and figures, or statues, is a form of art called sculpture. Sculpture is done in two ways: carving and molding. In carving, the sculptor cuts into a block of wood or stone with sharp tools. In molding, he makes a model in soft clay, then bakes the clay to harden it. From the hard model the sculptor makes a mold, and pours wet concrete or hot, liquid metal (such as bronze) into it. When this hardens, a perfect casting of the model is left.

Today, sculptors use all kinds of materials, including pieces of glass, metal, and cloth.

SEA

Some large areas of water around the edges of oceans are partly or completely surrounded by land, forming seas. The largest of them all is the South China Sea, part of the Pacific Ocean that lies between mainland China and Southeast Asia and the islands of Malaysia and the Philippines. Some seas, such as the Mediterranean, are almost completely cut off from the oceans they were once part of.

Large areas of water such as the Sea of Galilee, which were formed inland and were never part of an ocean, are also called seas.

SEA HORSE

The sea horse is actually a small sea fish. It gets its name from its horselike head. The sea horse swims in a peculiar upright position, fanning its dorsal (back) fin. It can cling onto seaweed, using its coiled tail.

Seal and Sea Lion: Seals and sea lions glide through the water, steering with their tails. Their bodies are streamlined to reduce water resistance.

SEAL AND SEA LION

These mammals spend most of their time in the sea. Their legs have become flippers, and they are expert swimmers. However, they have to come to the surface to breathe. Seals and sea lions catch fish under water. Seals swim by moving their bodies from side to side, using their front flippers like oars.

These animals come ashore to breed. They gather in large colonies on rocky coasts. Seals are slow and clumsy on land. But sea lions can turn their back flippers forward and move very quickly.

SEASONS

The different times of the year are called seasons. They are caused by the way the Earth orbits, or travels around the Sun. When the North Pole leans toward the Sun, northern lands have their summer

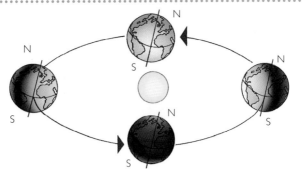

Seasons: *Seasons happen because the Earth is tilted as it orbits the Sun during the course of the year.*

and southern lands their winter. At the opposite point of the orbit, when the North Pole leans away from the Sun, northern lands have their winter and southern lands their summer. Spring and fall are the points in the orbit when the equator faces the Sun, so northern and southern lands have roughly the same amount of warmth.

Pea

Acorn

Seed: *Seeds are scattered in many different ways. Some, such as the maple, are carried by the wind.*

SEAWEED
See ALGAE.

SEED
Most plants reproduce themselves by means of seeds. They are formed in the plant's ovary. A seed contains an embryo—the plant in its earliest form. Seeds lie dormant or asleep until conditions are suitable for them to germinate. To germinate they need moisture, warmth, air, and darkness.

Maple

SENSES
Senses tell us what is happening around us and inside us. The external senses include hearing, taste, touch, sight, and smell. Each sense comes from nerve endings or sense organs, which send signals to our brain along the nervous system. For example, nerve endings on our tongue, called taste buds, tell us whether food is salty, sour, sweet, or bitter. Internal senses tell

us when we are hungry, tired, or thirsty. Muscle sense tells us the position of different parts of our body.

SEVEN WONDERS OF THE WORLD

Travelers in ancient times marveled at the Seven Wonders of the World. Of these, only the Pyramids can still be seen. The Lighthouse at Alexandria, the Colossus of Rhodes, the Statue of Zeus at Olympia, the Hanging Gardens of Babylon, the Temple of Artemis, and the Museum at Halicarnassus have all been destroyed.

SHAKESPEARE, WILLIAM (1564–1616)

Shakespeare is often called the world's greatest writer. He was born in Stratford-on-Avon, England. His plays are written in some of the most beautiful poetry in the English language. Some, such as *Richard II* and *Richard III*, are about history. Others, such as *A Midsummer Night's Dream*, are comedies. *Hamlet*, *Macbeth*, and *King Lear* are tragedies.

SHARK

Sharks are the most feared hunters of the sea. Drawn by the

Shark: *The mako shark is a fast, streamlined swimmer, whose speed allows it to attack large swordfish.*

smell of blood, they will kill fish, seals, porpoises, and even whales. Some sharks are man eaters, but most kinds are harmless to people.

Sharks are strong, fast-swimming fish. Their gaping jaws are full of sharp teeth. Instead of bones, sharks have cartilage skeletons.

SHEEP

Sheep are important farm animals. We make their wool into cloth, eat their meat, and wear their skins. Sheep feed on rough pasture, and their thick coats keep out bad weather. Wild sheep live in the mountains in parts of the Americas, Europe, and Asia.

SHIP

For at least 4,000 years ships have been sailing across seas. They still transport most of the world's

Galleon

Viking longship

Clipper

Steamer

Aircraft carrier

Supertanker

Cruise liner

Catamaran

Ship: *When the steam engine was invented, ships no longer relied on the wind.*

freight between the continents, but few carry passengers.

Until around a hundred years ago, most ships were propelled by sails. For many years, ships had only one square sail on a single mast. They could only sail well with the wind and relied on oars to propel them at other times. The Viking longships were an example of this.

By the 1400s, ships were built

with several masts, one of which carried a triangular fore and aft sail, which made sailing easier in all winds. Soon came the three-masted caravels and galleons. Last of the sailing ships were the graceful and speedy clippers, which were used to carry goods such as wool or tea from Australia and the Far East.

See also SUBMARINE.

SILICON CHIP

Silicon is the most common element after oxygen in the Earth's crust. Silicon chips are tiny pieces of silicon—as small as $^1/_{1000}$ sq. in.—made to carry minute electrical circuits, which are used in digital watches, electronic calculators, and computers.

See also COMPUTER.

SILK

The beautiful smooth cloth called silk is made from threads spun by the silkworm. This is actually the caterpillar of a moth. When the caterpillar is full-grown, it wraps itself in a cocoon of fine silk, stuck together with gum. The ancient Chinese were the first to discover how to wash away the gum and unwind the silk onto spools. It was then dyed and woven into cloth.

SILVER

Silver is a shiny metal that is used to make jewelry and expensive tableware. It can be shaped by bending and hammering.

Silver conducts (passes on) heat and electricity better than any other substance. It also forms compounds that are sensitive to light. These compounds are used in photography.

SKELETON

All the bones of your body make up your skeleton. The skeleton supports the soft parts of the body and is an anchor for the muscles. In vertebrates (animals with backbones), the skeleton is inside the body. Many invertebrates (animals without backbones) have an exoskeleton, which is like a hard crust on the outside of the body. Insects and spiders have exoskeletons.

SKIING

For thousands of years, skiing has been the main way to get around

Skeleton: *Adult humans have around 206 bones in their bodies.*

Skunk: The best-known skunk is the striped skunk, which is black with white markings on its back.

outer layer is the epidermis. It grows all the time, to replace dead skin cells that are rubbed off. Underneath the epidermis is a thicker layer called the dermis. It contains nerves and blood vessels. Hair grows out of it. The sweat glands are here too.

SKUNK

Skunks live in North America. They are relatives of badgers and weasels, and live in woodlands. They eat insects, birds' eggs, and small mammals. If attacked, the skunk raises its bushy tail and squirts out a foul-smelling spray of liquid from a special gland.

SLAVERY

Slaves are owned by people, and can be bought and sold as workers. In ancient Egypt, Greece, and Rome there were many slaves. Many of them died because their owners treated them so badly.

When Europeans started settling in America, they took slaves from Africa to work on the plantations. This slave trade was not stopped until the 1800s. All the slaves in the southern United States were freed in 1865 after the Civil War.

in deep snow. Skis from about 3000 B.C. have been found in Sweden. It is only during the last hundred years that skiing has been enjoyed as a sport. Ski racing and ski jumping were developed in Scandinavia around 1860. Downhill and slalom races are also international competitions.

SKIN

Skin is more than just the covering of the body. It helps prevent us from getting too hot or too cold. It helps keep out germs and helps the body get rid of waste.

The skin has two layers. The

SLEEP AND DREAMS

We spend around a third of our lives asleep. Our minds and bodies do not stop working while we sleep, but they do slow down.

Without sleep, we feel tired and grumpy, and we cannot concentrate.

Part of the brain is active during sleep. Though our eyelids are closed, our eyes move rapidly. When this happens, scientists know we are dreaming.

SLOTH

The slow-moving sloth lives in the South American forest. This strange mammal spends its life hanging upside down in trees. It eats leaves and fruit. The sloth's hooked claws are good for climbing, but useless for walking on the ground. The hair of the sloth hangs downward, so rainwater runs off easily. Sometimes algae grow on the hair, helping to hide the sloth from enemies such as the jaguar.

SNAKE

Snakes are legless reptiles. Unlike lizards, snakes have no eyelids. Most snakes lay eggs, but some give birth to live young.

All snakes prey on other animals, such as insects, birds, frogs, and small mammals. Poisonous snakes kill their prey by biting it with their fangs and injecting poison, or venom, into its body. Many snakes have no poison but grab their prey with their sharp teeth. Some large snakes, such as the python, coil their long bodies around their prey and crush it until it suffocates.

There are 2,500 different kinds of snakes, of which around 150 are dangerous to humans.

See also REPTILE.

SNOW AND SLEET

Inside a cloud there are millions of tiny water droplets. At the top, where the air is coldest, the water freezes to ice. Sometimes the drops of ice melt as they pass into warmer air and they fall as rain. But if the air is cold enough, they fall as snowflakes.

Snowflakes are tiny crystals. Each one has a beautiful pattern and always has six sides. A large snowflake is made of thousands of crystals stuck together.

Sleet is a mixture of snow and rain, and falls when the air is not quite warm enough to melt all the ice drops falling from the clouds.

See also RAIN AND HAIL.

Snake: *The poisonous coral snake is brightly colored as a warning.*

SOAP

Soap is a substance that helps wash away dirt and grease. The tiny soap particles are able to stick to and surround specks of dirt, and float them away in the water. Soap is made by boiling animal or vegetable fat with a chemical called an alkali.

Chemical cleaners called detergents are often used today instead of soap.

SOCCER

See FOOTBALL.

SOCIALISM

Socialism is a system of economics in which the central government operates state-owned industries and important natural resources. Such industries may include railroads, water, and gas companies. Unlike communists, socialists believe in a democratically elected government. Socialist ideals go back to the ancient Greek philosopher Plato. Today socialist ideas are applied by governments in many countries of the world.

SOCRATES (c.469–399 B.C.)

Socrates was an ancient Greek thinker and teacher. He developed the Socratic method, by which he used questions to help his students discover the answers they were seeking. One of his most famous pupils was Plato.

SOIL

A handful of garden soil does not look very interesting. But it is alive with millions of tiny plants and animals that help to keep soil fertile. Soil is made from crumbled rocks. The process of wearing down rocks into small pieces takes millions of years. When plants and animals die, their remains are broken down by bacteria into humus. Humus holds moisture in the soil and binds the soil together. Fertile soil holds a lot of water and air.

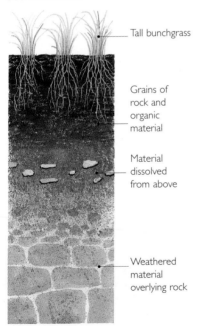

Tall bunchgrass

Grains of rock and organic material

Material dissolved from above

Weathered material overlying rock

Soil: Soils have three distinct layers, or horizons, between the surface of the earth and the rock below.

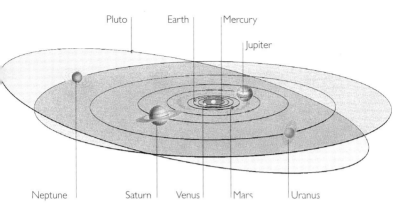

Pluto | Earth | Mercury | Jupiter

Neptune | Saturn | Venus | Mars | Uranus

Solar System: *The planets go around the Sun in elliptical orbits, which means that they follow a path like a flattened circle.*

SOLAR SYSTEM

The solar system consists of the Sun and all the heavenly bodies in orbit around it. The Sun's great mass exerts a gravitational pull that keeps the planets, their satellites, comets, and asteroids moving around it.

Planets are small celestial bodies that circle around the Sun. Unlike stars, planets do not produce their own light. They shine because they reflect the Sun's light. There are nine planets circling the Sun: Mercury (the planet nearest to the Sun), Venus, Earth, Mars, Jupiter, Saturn, Uranus, Neptune, and Pluto. There may be other planets beyond Pluto that still have yet to be discovered.

The planets can be divided into two groups, gaseous and rocky. The Earth is the biggest of the rocky planets, which also include Mercury, Venus, Mars, and Pluto. The other planets consist mainly of gases. Saturn, Jupiter, Uranus, and Neptune are surrounded by rings of gas and dust.

The planets are not the only bodies orbiting around the Sun. There are also the asteroids, sometimes known as the minor planets. They are much smaller than planets—the largest are a few hundred miles across. Around 2,000 asteroids have already been recorded, and more are being discovered all the time.

All of the planets except Mercury and Venus have their own satellites orbiting around them— the Moon is Earth's only satellite.

The Earth is the only known planet on which life can exist. Mercury and Venus are too hot for life to exist. And the outer planets are too cold. It is possible that some kind of life could exist on Mars. But there are other planets in the universe, circling around other suns.

SOUND

Sound is produced by objects that are vibrating to and fro. If you pluck a violin string and touch it, you can feel it vibrating. A vibrating string gently nudges the molecules around it. These air molecules nudge other air molecules and a wave spreads from the string through the air, like ripples spread on a pond.

When the sound wave strikes our ears, it causes our tympanic membrane to vibrate and nerves to send signals to the brain. This is how we hear. If there were no air, there would be nothing to carry the sound. That is why there is no sound in space.

Sounds are described in various ways. They can be loud or soft; high or low. High sounds, or rather, high-pitched sounds, are made by things that vibrate rapidly. Low-pitched sounds are made by slow vibrations.

Some things produce sound waves pitched too high for us to hear. We call these waves ultrasonic.

SOUTH AFRICA

The Republic of South Africa lies at the southern end of Africa. It is a warm, sunny land and many wild animals roam in its huge national parks. But there are also large cities, such as Johannesburg, Cape Town, and Durban. South Africa is a rich country. Farming and mining (for gold, diamonds, and uranium) are the main activities.

Although most South Africans are black, Indian, or of mixed race, the races lived separately under the apartheid system for many years. This was finally abolished by the government in 1991.

SOUTH AMERICA

There are 13 countries in South America. At 6,800,000 sq. mi., it is the fourth-largest continent in the world. It has dense rain forests, barren deserts, wide grasslands, and high mountains.

The Andes Mountains, the highest in all of South America, stretch for more than 4,400 miles down the western side. In the center of the continent are vast plains. They include the forests of the Amazon basin, which cover an area the size of western Europe, and the grassy pampas of Argentina.

South America is rich in minerals, such as copper, tin, iron, bauxite, diamonds, and emeralds. Mining is an important industry everywhere, and there are also large oil fields, particularly off the coast of Venezuela.

Space Exploration: The space shuttle can take off like a rocket but land like a glider, and may be used many times.

Today, South America is a rapidly changing continent. Until recently many of its governments were controlled by military leaders, but more are democratic now.

See also ARGENTINA; BRAZIL; INCAS; PAGE 62.

SOUTHEAST ASIA

Southeast Asia includes Brunei, Myanmar, Singapore, the Philippines, Malaysia, Indonesia, Cambodia, Laos, Vietnam, and Thailand. It has forested mountains, broad river valleys, volcanic regions, low plains, and palm-fringed beaches. Its tropical climate with monsoon rains makes it an ideal rice-growing area.

The main industries are agricultural, although manufacturing industries also thrive in the cities. The region's main exports include rice, oil and petroleum products, rubber, coconut and palm oil, electronic equipment, timber, and tin.

All of the countries except Thailand were part of European empires but gained independence during the 1900s. Many countries fell under military rule, and oppression continues today. Vietnam, Cambodia, and Laos were all involved in the Vietnam War in the 1960s and 1970s that greatly damaged their economies and environment. A lot has been done since to repair the damage, and both tourism and trade are steadily developing.

SPACE EXPLORATION

The Russians launched the first spacecraft, *Sputnik I*, in October 1957. The first man went into space in April 1961, when the Russian Yuri Gagarin flew once around the Earth. Americans put the first men on the Moon in July 1969.

Today many spacecraft are being sent into space. Some, such as satellites and probes, are unmanned. Satellites carry equipment such as measuring instruments, tape recorders, radios, and cameras. Probes are sent to explore the Moon and planets. Probes have already photographed all the planets out to Neptune, and have landed on Venus and Mars.

The space shuttle is the first reusable spacecraft. Launched into space by a rocket, the winged orbiter goes into its path around the Earth. When its mission is complete, the orbiter is slowed until it drops out of orbit. Once back inside Earth's atmosphere, the astronauts maneuver the shuttle like a glider, bringing it to a landing on a runway.

See also ASTRONAUT; SATELLITE.

SPAIN AND PORTUGAL
Spain and Portugal are in southwestern Europe. Much of the center of Spain is a high plateau that is dry and dusty. The north is green and fertile, while the south is hot and dry. Portugal lies on the Atlantic coast to the west of Spain. It is rocky, mild, and damp in the north, but flat and very hot in the south.

Many Spaniards work in industries such as car manufacturing, catering, and tourism, and many others are farmers, producing goods such as olives, oranges, and onions. One of Portugal's main exports is cork, and both countries are famed for their wines and ports.

In the 1400s, Spain and Portugal built up a huge empire, mainly in South America, but they lost their power throughout the 1600s.

During the 1900s, both countries were ruled by harsh dictators, but became democracies in the 1970s.

SPECTRUM
The band of colors that we see in a rainbow, from red to violet, is called the spectrum of colors. White light is made up of all the colors of the rainbow, which can

Spider: *The black widow is one of the few spiders that are poisonous to humans. There are around 30,000 different kinds of spiders.*

be seen when we put a triangle-shaped block of glass called a prism in front of a beam of ordinary white light.

The spectrum of light in turn is just one section of the electromagnetic spectrum. This includes all forms of radiation, including radio waves, microwaves, infrared rays, light waves, ultraviolet rays, X-rays, and gamma rays.

SPIDER

Spiders may look like insects but they are not. Their bodies are made up of two parts (not three) and they have eight legs (not six). They are related to scorpions.

All spiders make silk inside their bodies. Some spiders use the silk to make webs to trap insects for food. However, not all spiders build webs. Wolf spiders chase their prey on the ground. Crab spiders lurk inside flowers, while trap-door spiders lie in wait in holes.

STALACTITE AND STALAGMITE

These are two types of mineral deposits found in caves. Stalactites grow downward from the roof. Stalagmites grow up from the floor of the cave and can be as much as 100 feet high.

Both are formed by water that seeps into the caves and drips from the limestone ceilings. The water is often saturated with dissolved

Stalactite and Stalagmite:
As water drips into a limestone cave, lime deposits may come out of the solution to form a rocky "icicle."

minerals that are then deposited in iciclelike formations. Stalactites and stalagmites are sometimes called dripstones.

See also CAVE.

STALIN, JOSEPH (1879–1953)

Stalin was a revolutionary leader who worked to overthrow the Czar of Russia in 1917. As leader of the Soviet Union from 1924 to his death, he helped to turn Russia into an industrialized state. But Stalin was responsible for millions of deaths, and in 1956 he was denounced as a dictator.

STAMP

Postage stamps were first used in Britain in 1840. They were the idea of a man called Rowland Hill. To keep stamps from being used twice, the post office cancels them with an ink postmark. This shows where and when the letter was posted.

See also POST OFFICE.

STAR

The stars we see in the night sky are balls of glowing gases. They are so far away that they seem very tiny, but if we could get closer they would look like the Sun. Stars shine by nuclear power: heat and light produced when atoms of hydrogen gas fuse, or join together.

Astronomers are not sure how stars originated, but many think that they are formed out of great clouds of cool dust and gases.

See also NUCLEAR ENERGY; SUN; UNIVERSE.

STEAM ENGINE

James Watt built the first truly efficient steam engines in the late 1700s, and made them suitable for driving machinery of all kinds.

In Watt's type of engine, steam pushes a piston back and forth in a cylinder. The piston is connected to whatever is to be driven—for example, the wheels of a locomotive. Steam is produced by burning coal or wood in a furnace beneath a boiler. The hot gases from the furnace pass through tubes in the boiler and heat the water. The steam that is produced drives the pistons.

STONE AGE

This is the name given to the period before people learned to obtain and use metal. Tools and weapons were made from flint and other rocks and wood. The Stone Age probably began about three million years ago.

There are three Stone Age periods: the Old (Paleolithic), Middle (Mesolithic), and the New (Neolithic).

At the beginning of the Old Stone Age, hunters made clumsy stone axes. Thousands of

Steam Engine: James Watt designed this rotary steam engine in 1783.

years passed before they could chip flint into double-edged blades to make more effective implements: knives, scrapers, and weapons.

Middle Stone Age people made more intricate tools and weapons. Many were set in wooden or bone hafts and handles, making them easier to use.

Farming replaced hunting in the New Stone Age. Tools became more refined and more specialized for a particular task.

See also BRONZE AGE; IRON AGE.

SUBMARINE

Ships that can travel underwater are called submarines. A submarine dives by letting water into tanks around the hull (body). This makes it heavier than water. To surface, it blows the water out, making it lighter again.

Ordinary submarines are propelled underwater by a propeller driven by electric batteries. They have to surface when their batteries run down. On the water they are propelled by diesel engines, which also charge the batteries. Nuclear submarines are powered by a

Submarine: At 560 feet long, the Russian Typhoons are the world's biggest submarines.

nuclear reactor. They can remain underwater for months at a time.

The crew of a submarine use a periscope to see above the surface of the water. A periscope is an instrument that can also be used to see over walls and around corners.

SUGAR

Plants make sugar for their own food. The sugar that we use to sweeten food is called sucrose. It comes from sugar beet and sugarcane. Other sugars are fructose (from fruit), glucose (from fruit, vegetables, and grain), and lactose (from milk).

Sugar is a very important food because it supplies energy and heat, and helps to form fat.

SUN

The Sun is our nearest star. It is a great ball of very hot gases swirling in space. All the time it pours out heat and light, as atoms of hydrogen gas join together inside it to form atoms of another gas—helium. Life on Earth

Sun: *Our Sun is a fiercely hot globe of burning gas, mainly hydrogen, measuring nearly a million miles across.*

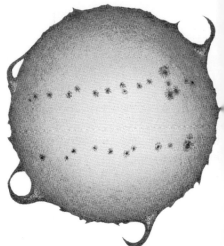

depends on this heat and light. Without it, the Earth would be a dark, cold, dead lump of rock. All living things need warmth, and plants need sunlight to make food.

The Sun is like many other stars in the sky. It appears bigger and hotter because it is nearer than the other stars. The Earth is part of the Sun's family, or solar system. It is one of nine planets circling around the Sun.

See also SOLAR SYSTEM; STAR.

SWITZERLAND AND AUSTRIA

Switzerland and Austria, in central Europe, are bordered by the Alps. They are both lands of mountains, forests, lakes, and green pastures. Apart from producing hydroelectric power from its rivers, Switzerland has few natural resources. It is a world center of banking. Austria produces timber, iron ore, lead, and copper, and also manufactures steel and paper. Both countries have thriving tourist industries, especially for winter sports.

Switzerland has remained a neutral country, keeping out of European wars since 1815. This has attracted the offices of many organizations that depend on international cooperation, such as the United Nations.

SYNAGOGUE

Synagogues are the center of Jewish religious life, and are used for worship, meetings, and study. Synagogues are built in many styles, but they all contain an ark, an ornately decorated chest where a copy of the Torah (Jewish law) is kept, with a light constantly burning in front of it.

They have a raised platform, the bema, where people stand to conduct services and read the scriptures, and pews, where the leaders of the community sit. Other people stand.

TALMUD

The Talmud is one of the holy books of Judaism. It is a collection of ancient writings that includes many of the laws that govern everyday life for Jewish people and interprets these laws. The Talmud and the Torah, the other holy book of Judaism, contain the religious and political laws of Jewish people, wherever they live.

TANK

A tank is a large, armored military vehicle on a continuous "caterpillar" track that allows it to travel over rough ground. It was first used by Britain during World War I. At the top of the tank is a rotating gun turret. The crew is protected inside the body of the tank. Tanks were used during World War II, both by the Germans in their *blitzkriegs* (lightning attacks) and in Allied landing operations in Europe and the Pacific.

See also WAR.

TAX

The government needs money to run the country. It gets this money mainly from the taxes we pay. Taxes pay for the roads, schools, hospitals, and many other services a country needs.

There are several kinds of taxes. Most people pay tax on their income—the money they earn. Income tax is a direct tax. Property tax is another form of direct tax. Indirect taxes are taxes on goods and services. Tariffs are taxes that are paid when goods enter the country. Excise taxes are added to goods such as tobacco and alcohol.

Tank: *The American M-60 was developed after World War II.*

TEA

Tea is made by pouring boiling water onto tea leaves. The leaves come from tea bushes, which are grown mainly in India, Sri Lanka, and China. Tea first came to Europe from China in the 1600s. At first it was brewed and stored in barrels, like beer.

TEETH

Teeth cut and chew food into pieces small enough to be swallowed. The kinds of teeth an animal has depends on the kind of food it eats.

Beasts of prey, such as wolves and lions, have long, sharp teeth. They use them to kill their prey and to tear the meat. Rodents, such as squirrels, have gnawing teeth. Grazing animals, such as cattle, have flat grinding teeth.

Human beings have sharp

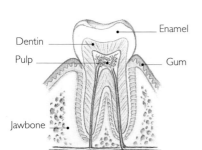

Dentin
Enamel
Pulp
Gum
Jawbone

Teeth: *Molars are located at the back of the mouth and are used for grinding food.*

Telescope: *The way light passes through glass affects how we see objects, whether through a magnifying lens, a camera lens, or a telescope.*

cutting teeth and flat grinding teeth. This is because we eat both meat and plants.

TELEPHONE

The first telephone calls could only be sent through wires. Now a telephone call may travel by wire, or by radio, sometimes bounced off satellites. When you dial a number, the telephone sends out electrical pulses. They go to an exchange, which automatically connects you to the number you dialed.

When you talk, a microphone changes your voice into electrical signals. These travel down the wires to the earpiece of the person you are talking to. There they are changed back into the sound of your voice.

TELESCOPE

A telescope is an instrument that makes distant objects appear nearer and larger.

The simplest type, refractors, consist of a tube containing two lenses, which bend the light rays from the distant object and make it appear closer.

Most astronomers, however, use reflectors, which have a mirror to collect and bend the light. They are bigger and clearer than refractors.

Astronomers also use radio telescopes: large metal dishes that gather radio waves sent out by heavenly bodies.

Television: The receiver's TV antenna picks up signals sent from the transmitter.

TELEVISION

"Television" means "pictures from a distance." Television can show us live pictures of events on the other side of the world.

Two important pieces of television equipment are the camera and the receiver. The camera records an image of a scene on an electrically charged plate. A beam of electrons then sweeps back and forth across this plate. The result is electric signals that represent the brightness in different parts of the scene. These signals are combined with a radio wave and sent out by a transmitter.

The antenna of the television set picks up the wave. Circuits in the set separate the signal from the wave. These signals then go to the picture tube where a "gun" fires a beam of electrons at the screen, causing a spot of light. The signals alter the strength of the beam and thereby the brightness of the spot. They also make the beam sweep back and forth in a series of lines of spots of varying brightness. The lines are very close together, and we see them as a complete picture.

TENNIS

When we use the word "tennis" we are usually referring to the game of lawn tennis. It is played on hard or grass courts. Two people play in a singles match; four people in a doubles match.

Theater: William Shakespeare's Globe Theatre was built in London in 1599.

Tennis today is a form of an old French game.

TERRORISM

Revolutionary groups, guerrilla fighters, and other extremist groups who cannot get what they want in peaceful ways sometimes use terrorism—acts of terror and violence carried out against the public, such as bombing, kidnapping, and hijacking airplanes and ships—to try to make governments give them what they want, or to overthrow a government altogether. Some terrorists are fighting for political or religious freedom at home; others use terrorism as a way to attack foreign countries.

THEATER

The first theaters were in ancient Greece. People sat in the open air on a hillside, while actors and dancers performed on a space below called the orchestra. Behind the actors was a changing room called the skene. This later became a stage, and it gives us the modern words "scenery" and "scene." England's first theaters were built in the 1500s. Each had a jutting stage almost surrounded by the audience. Rich

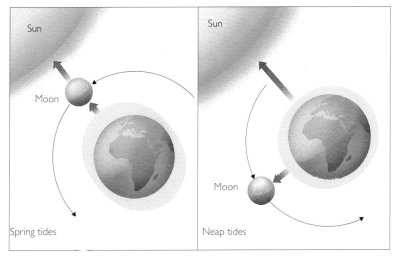

Spring tides

Neap tides

Tides: Spring tides are high, because the Sun's gravitational pull is combined with the Moon's. Neap tides are the lowest.

people sat under cover. Poor spectators stood in the uncovered "pit." But soon all theaters had roofs. Complicated scenery and stage machinery started to be used. And, to hide the workings from the audience, a "picture frame" was put around the stage. The audience now only sat in front of it. Some modern theaters have gone back to the old idea.

See also PLAY.

THERMOMETER

A thermometer measures temperature—how hot or cold it is.

Most thermometers consist of a thin tube with a bulb of liquid. When liquids are heated, they expand, or grow bigger. So when the liquid in the bulb becomes hotter, it rises up the tube. The liquid used is generally mercury or colored alcohol. A gas thermometer uses the effect of heat on gas.

Every thermometer has a scale marked on it. The two scales used are the Fahrenheit scale, or the Celsius (or centigrade) scale.

THUNDER

See LIGHTNING AND THUNDER.

TIDES

Tides are caused by the Moon and the Sun pulling the world's oceans toward them. This is the result of gravity. Because the Moon is closer to Earth than the Sun is, its pull is stronger.

There are around two high tides and two low tides every 24 hours. When the Moon and Sun are on the same side of the Earth—at new and full Moon—their combined pull produces the biggest tides, called spring tides. When the Moon and Sun are pulling at right angles to each other, the smallest tides, called neap tides, occur.

Tiger: A tigress watches over her two cubs as they play.

TIGER

The tiger is the largest of the big cats. Its home is Asia. Most tigers live in hot forests, but the largest come from cold Siberia.

Tigers hunt alone and at night. They prey on deer, wild cattle, and pigs. Only an old or sick tiger will attack people. The tiger's stripes camouflage it in long grass.

TIME

The day is a natural unit of time. It is the time the Earth takes to spin around once in space. Our other main natural unit of time is the year—the time it takes the Earth to travel once around the Sun. There are 365¼ days in a year.

The Moon circles the Earth every 27 days. This gives us another unit of time—the month. Our calendar has 12 months in each year.

We measure time, or the passage of time, with clocks and watches. They help us split each day into 24 hours; each hour into 60 minutes; and each minute into 60 seconds. Day, hour, minute, and second are units of time. We can say what time it is in two ways—by a 12-hour clock or a 24-hour clock.

See also CALENDAR; CLOCK AND WATCH.

TIN

Tin is a common but very important metal. It resists corrosion (being eaten away) by acids and is often used for protective coatings, such as on the inside of cans of food. Its most important use is in alloys such as bronze and brass.

TOBACCO

Tobacco is made from the dried leaves of the tobacco plant. It originally grew wild in the

Americas. The Spaniards brought tobacco to Europe in the 1500s, and today tobacco is grown in Asia, Africa, and Europe as well as the Americas.

Tobacco leaf can be made into pipe, cigar, or cigarette tobacco, or snuff. Smoking is a harmful habit. It is particularly bad for the lungs and heart.

TRANSISTOR

A transistor is a small electronic device used to amplify or to strengthen signals in electronic equipment such as radios, computers, and satellites. It is made from crystals of material such as germanium or silicon.

Transistors were invented in 1948. A large number of them can be put in a silicon chip the size of a pinhead.

See also SILICON CHIP.

TREE

Trees are the largest of all plants. The world's biggest tree is the Californian redwood, which can reach a height of more than 330 feet. Trees grow a little each year. The tips of their branches grow longer, and a ring of tissue in the trunk and the older branches creates more cells to make them thicker.

Evergreen trees keep their leaves all year round. Conifers, such as spruce, pine, and fir, are evergreens. They grow in colder climates. Their leaves are thin and hard, and look like needles. Conifers do not have flowers;

Larch

Oak

Tree: *The leaves and fruit (cones) of the European larch, a conifer, are very different from those of the deciduous oak.*

215

instead, they have winged seeds hidden inside cones.

Many tropical trees are also evergreens. But they have broad leaves, and flowers. Broad-leaved trees grow in cool countries too. Those that shed their leaves in the fall are called deciduous.

TUNNEL

Ever since prehistoric people enlarged their caves, humans have invented ways to tunnel out underground passageways. Today, tunnels are constructed under mountains, seas, and cities, mainly for roads and railroads and for providing services such as water and sewers.

Automatic tunneling machines can be used on soft or hard rocks. They have a rotating, drilling head and a conveyor belt to carry back the earth and rock. Some tunnels are dug out from ground level. Then the tunnel walls are built

Tunnel: The automatic tunnel-digging machines used today are called moles. They have rotating cutters at the front and a conveyor belt to carry away the rock or soil.

Conveyor belt   Cutting head

and the tunnel is covered.
Underwater tunnels are
sometimes made from sections of
tubing that are positioned in a
trench, which is then filled in
again around the tunnel.

TURKEY
See GREECE AND TURKEY.

TURKEY
The turkey is a game bird,
and is traditionally served at
Thanksgiving and Christmas. The
wild turkey is native to North
American woodlands. Benjamin
Franklin once proposed that the
turkey be the national bird of
the U.S. During the congressional
vote on the issue, the turkey was
beaten by the bald eagle.

TURTLE AND TORTOISE
Unlike other reptiles, turtles and
tortoises have hard shells to
protect their bodies.

Turtles live in the sea. They
have flatter shells than tortoises,
and use their legs as paddles for

*Turtle and Tortoise: A snapping
turtle can bite off a person's fingers
with its powerful jaws.*

swimming. On land they tend to
be very clumsy.

Tortoises are land animals.
They live in warm countries and
eat plant food. A tortoise cannot
run away from an enemy.
Instead, it tucks its head and legs
into its shell. Some tortoises can
live to be much more than one
hundred years old—which is
older than any other animal.

See also REPTILE.

TWAIN, MARK (1835–1910)
The great American novelist and
travel writer, Mark Twain, was
born Samuel Langhorne
Clemens. He grew up on the
Mississippi River and later wrote
about life on the Mississippi. His
best-known works include *The
Adventures of Tom Sawyer* and
*The Adventures of Huckleberry
Finn*, both based on his
experiences as a boy.

U

ULTRAVIOLET RAYS

Light from the Sun can be split by a prism into a spectrum of color. Red is at one end of the spectrum, and violet is at the other. Ultraviolet rays are found beyond the violet end of the spectrum.

These rays are very useful and important, although we cannot see them. They produce vitamin D in our bodies, which is necessary for growing healthy bones and teeth. Ultraviolet rays can also be used to kill bacteria.

UNION, LABOR

Labor unions are organizations or associations of workers. By joining together in a union, workers can more easily negotiate, or bargain, with their employers for higher wages or better working conditions. Each industry has its own union.

UNITED KINGDOM

See BRITISH ISLES.

UNITED NATIONS

There have been two terrible world wars in the 1900s, and after each of them a special organization has been set up to try to prevent another such war from breaking out.

The League of Nations was formed after World War I. The United States never joined it and this weakened the League. Gradually other nations dropped out.

Despite the League's failure, it served as a model when the United Nations (UN) was founded after World War II in 1945. The UN still exists and tries to settle quarrels between countries peacefully. It helps refugees and children, and sends experts to fight hunger, disease, and ignorance in poor countries. The UN headquarters are in New York City. Here, the General Assembly and the Security Council meet to discuss world problems.

United Nations: *The flag of the UN shows a map of the world surrounded by an olive wreath.*

UNITED STATES OF AMERICA

United States of America: The faces of four U.S. presidents are carved on a granite cliff at Mt. Rushmore, South Dakota.

Fifty states make up the United States of America. This huge country consists of continental North America, Alaska in the far north, and Hawaii in the Pacific Ocean.

The climate varies from region to region. Some areas are hot in summer and cold in winter, but the south and west coasts have mild winters.

The United States has many natural resources. Its farmland is fertile. Huge crops of wheat are grown on the prairies, and corn, tobacco, cotton, fruit, and vegetables are also grown. From the forests comes timber, while underground are valuable minerals, including coal, oil, natural gas, iron, gold, copper, and uranium. Many rivers and lakes have been dammed to produce electricity.

More than half the people live in towns and cities; the United States is the greatest industrial country in the world. Its factories make aircraft, automobiles, computers, machines, and many other kinds of goods.

The first Americans were the Native Americans, who lived by farming and hunting. But after Columbus's discovery of the "New World," Europeans started to settle in North America. Starting in the

Universe: The universe is made up of galaxies, stars, planets, moons, asteroids, and other bodies scattered throughout space.

1600s, the British set up 13 colonies on the east coast. But the colonists wanted to govern themselves, and in 1776 they declared themselves independent from Britain and became a republic. The republic grew into a union of 50 states. Many people from around the world came to the United States to enjoy freedom and opportunity.

UNIVERSE

When we talk of the universe, we mean everything that exists. This includes the air, the sea, the Earth, the other planets, the Moon, the stars, and space.

Years ago, people thought that the Earth was the center of the universe, and that all the other heavenly bodies circled around it. Around 500 years ago, people started to realize that the Earth was not the center. Now we know that the Earth is only a tiny speck in the universe. It belongs to the Sun's family of stars called the galaxy. The galaxy belongs to a family of galaxies, and there are millions of these families in the universe. Most of the universe is just empty space, however.

URANIUM

This element is a rare metal. It is radioactive—it gives off invisible rays that will darken film.

Discovered in 1789, uranium had very few uses until 1940. Then a way of getting energy from it was discovered. When uranium is bombarded with neutrons, its atoms become unstable. They split and give off energy. This is called fission. Uranium is used for nuclear power and in atomic bombs.

See also NUCLEAR ENERGY.

V

VEGETABLE

Many of the plants we eat are called vegetables. Vegetables are good food, supplying energy or bodybuilding substances.

Various parts of vegetables are eaten. Potatoes, carrots, and turnips are root vegetables; spinach is a leaf; brussels sprouts are leaf buds; and broccoli is a flower. Some fruit and seeds are eaten as vegetables. Tomatoes and cucumbers are fruit; peas and beans are seeds.

Vegetable: We eat a vegetable's leaf, stem, root, seed, or fruit.

Victoria: Queen Victoria presided over the British Empire.

VICTORIA (1819–1901)

Queen Victoria reigned for 64 years—longer than any other British monarch. She became queen when she was only 18. Victoria loved her husband, Prince

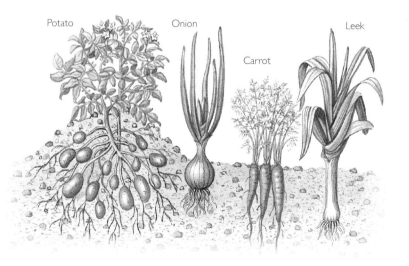

Potato   Onion   Carrot   Leek

Albert, very dearly. After he died in 1861, she spent the rest of her life in mourning. During her reign (1837–1901), Britain grew to be a mighty industrial nation, ruling a huge empire.

VIDEOTAPE

Videotape allows us to record sound and pictures on tape. Many television programs are recorded on videotape to be sent across a network or for relaying at a later time.

Home videos are now very popular. Some of these are prerecorded tapes of films or video games that can be played on a videocassette recorder (VCR) attached to a television set. Others are blank tapes that can be used to record television programs.

VIKING

In the eighth century, fierce Viking from Scandinavia started to raid th coasts of western Europe. They burned villages, robbed churches, stole cattle, and carried off slaves. People were terrified of them, especially as Vikings often fought like madmen, as if they were eager to die in battle.

But the Vikings were not simply pirates and robbers. They were also farmers and tradesmen. Their craftsmen were highly skilled in using iron, gold, and silver. And their sagas tell the story of their legendary exploits.

In their longships (wooden boats with oars and square sails) they

Viking: Olaf, King of Norway, was killed in a sea battle in A.D. 1000.

crossed the Atlantic Ocean to settle in Iceland and Greenland. They probably reached North America around A.D. 1000. The Vikings also settled in Ireland, France, Russia, and England.

VITAMIN

Vitamins are chemicals that our bodies need for healthy growth. We get vitamins from food. Vitamin A comes from lettuce, carrots, butter, and eggs. It helps us grow. There are several kinds of Vitamin B. We eat them in cereals, milk, meat, vegetables, and fruit. Vitamin C is found in fruit and prevents us from getting a disease called scurvy. Vitamin D is important to babies: it prevents a bone disease called rickets. Egg yolk, fish oils, margarine, and liver are rich in vitamin D. Sunlight has the same effect. Other vitamins are known as E and K. The body only uses vitamins in tiny quantities. A good varied diet gives it all the vitamins it needs.

VOLCANO

Volcanoes occur where the Earth's crust is being squeezed or stretched as new mountains are formed. The enormous pressures inside the Earth melt the solid rock to liquid magma. When the pressures become too great, gases and hot liquid rock, called lava, may burst through the center of a volcano and out of a pit or crater at the top.

Volcanoes are usually cone-shaped with a crater at the top. Active volcanoes erupt for short periods and then remain dormant for long periods. If the lava remains bubbling in a lava lake, eruptions are just overflows. If, however, the lava solidifies and blocks the top of the volcano, the next eruption will explode.

Volcano: Hot lava and molten rock spout up from the central vent. The mountain is made from layers of cold ash and lava.

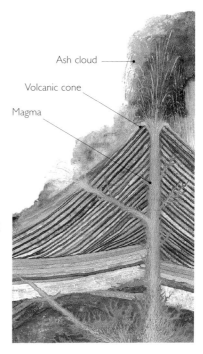

Ash cloud

Volcanic cone

Magma

223

WAR

People have always found it difficult to live together in peace. From prehistoric times, envy and greed have made one tribe attack another, in order to steal its land or animals. Later, great empires were founded by conquering armies.

In ancient Greece and Rome, soldiers were armed with swords, spears, and bows and arrows. Infantry, soldiers on foot, made up the largest part of an army.

Cavalry, soldiers on horseback, played an important part in wars throughout the Middle Ages. Knights in armor, armed with lances, swords and clubs, battered their way through enemy ranks.

Gunpowder came into use in the 1300s. From then on, wars were fought increasingly with guns. But it took many years before soldiers had guns light enough to carry easily.

By 1914, guns were so powerful that soldiers had to dig trenches for protection. During World War I whole armies were bogged down in trenches.

World War II was fought in Europe, Africa, and Asia. Most of the world's leading nations took part.

See also CIVIL WAR; WORLD WAR I; WORLD WAR II.

WASHINGTON, GEORGE (1732–1799)

George Washington, the first president of the United States was a farmer from Virginia. When the colonists fought the British in the American Revolution from 1775 to 1783, Washington became general of the army. In 1789, he became president, although he did not consider himself fit for such an important task.

MAJOR WARS

Some of the most important wars fought since the fall of the Roman Empire in A.D. 476.

1337–1453	Hundred Years' War
1455–1485	Wars of the Roses
1618–1648	Thirty Years' War
1642–1651	English Civil War
1701–1713	War of Spanish Succession
1740–1748	War of Austrian Succession
1756–1763	Seven Years' War
1775–1783	American Revolution
1792–1815	Napoleonic Wars
1846–1848	Mexican War
1854–1856	Crimean War
1861–1865	American Civil War
1870–1871	Franco-Prussian War
1914–1918	World War I
1939–1945	World War II
1950–1953	Korean War
1957–1975	Vietnam War
1973	Yom Kippur War
1980–1988	Iran–Iraq War
1991	Gulf War

WASP
See BEE AND WASP.

WATER
Water is the most precious liquid on Earth; without it, nothing can live. Water consists of hydrogen and oxygen. Its molecules contain two atoms of hydrogen (H) to one atom of oxygen (O). We write this as the chemical formula H_2O.

Water plays an important part in our weather. The Sun warms the Earth's water, changing some of it into vapor. The vapor rises and, as it does so, condenses and falls as rain or snow. This continuous process is called the water cycle.

Water also shapes the Earth. Rain, ocean waves, and rivers erode the land. Glaciers gouge paths through rocks and soil.

Huge dams can harness the power of water to make electricity. We call this form of power hydroelectricity.

See also ENERGY; GLACIER; LAKE; OCEAN; RAIN AND HAIL; RIVER.

Wave: At sea, waves are caused mainly by the wind.

WATERFALL
A waterfall is caused by water wearing away rock at different speeds. If a river flows over a join between hard rock and soft rock, it wears away the soft rock more quickly and makes a deep "step." Some waterfalls are very small, but in other places wide rivers fall over huge cliffs. The most famous falls are the Niagara Falls, between Canada and the United States, and the Victoria Falls in Africa.

WATT, JAMES (1736–1819)
Watt was a Scottish engineer, who invented a more efficient steam engine than any before. He devised a condenser and several methods of changing the motion of a piston into the rotating motion of a wheel.

WAVE
If you drop a stone into a pond, it pushes the water out of the way in a wave. The energy in this wave moves along to make another wave, and in this way moves across the water. Sound is also carried by waves. Light waves,

Wind direction

Crest of wave

Trough of wave

X-rays, radio waves, and other forms of radiation are all types of electromagnetic waves.

Whale: The blue whale is the largest whale and the largest mammal ever to live.

WEATHER

The Earth's atmosphere moves constantly, driven by the Sun's heat. Huge masses of warm and cold air flow between the tropics and the polar regions. As these air masses meet, rise and fall, and heat and cool, they cause weather. The meeting line between a cold and warm air mass is called a front. Fronts usually bring changes in the weather such as clouds, rain, or stroms. Cold fronts cause sudden changes in weather; warm fronts cause gradual changes.

WEST INDIES

See CARIBBEAN.

WHALE

Although whales spend all their lives in the sea, they are mammals, not fish. Whales are warm-blooded. They have skin, not scales. The females give birth to live young and feed them on milk. A whale can dive to great depths, loading its blood with enough oxygen to last for up to 45 minutes, but it must surface to breathe. Whales swim by beating their tails up and down.

There are two families of whales: toothed whales, and whalebone or baleen whales.

WHEEL

The wheel is one of the most important inventions. A great deal of human and animal energy is saved through using it.

Nobody knows when the wheel was invented. Its first use was probably as a potter's wheel in Mesopotamia around 5,000 years ago. Wheels were next used on carts. These wheels were solid, made by cutting slices off large tree trunks.

Without wheels, advanced transportation systems would be impossible. They are essential to most machines and engines.

WILLIAM THE CONQUEROR
(*c.*1027–1087)
In 1066, William, Duke of Normandy, landed with his army in Sussex and defeated and killed King Harold. He was crowned William I, the first Norman king of England.

William was an efficient administrator. He caused a great survey of the land to be made. It is known as the Domesday Book. William's descendants ruled England for many years after his death.

WIND
Wind is the movement of air over the Earth's surface. The main cause of wind is the unequal heating of the Earth's surface. At the equator, which gets most heat from the Sun, air becomes warm and rises. At the poles, which are the coldest places, cold air sinks. As the warm air rises, cool air moves in to take its place. Changing temperatures over the sea and land also affect the pattern of the winds.

Winds are named after the direction from which they come, so a north wind blows from the north, and so on.

Wheel: From the first time humans ever rolled a log to the pneumatic (air-filled) tires of today, the wheel has traveled a long way.

WINDMILL
Windmills are used to pump water, generate electricity, and grind corn. Their source of power is the wind. Sails or vanes are fixed to a shaft. The shaft is connected to the machinery to be driven. As other forms of energy become expensive, windmills may again become popular. A light steel type has been

Windmill: The most efficient modern wind machines have two or three vanes like an aircraft propeller.

devised in the United States for use on farms.

WOOD

Wood is used in building, making furniture, and is burned as fuel. Cut wood is called timber. The timber we get from coniferous trees, such as pine, is called softwood. The timber we get from deciduous trees, such as oak, is called hardwood. Softwoods are used mainly in building construction; hardwoods, for furniture.

Wood is also made into paper, textile fibers, plastics, explosives, and several other chemicals. The main chemical substance in wood is cellulose.

WOOL

Wool is the fine hair from the fleece of sheep. Wool fibers are naturally crinkled, which helps woolen garments to keep their shape. Each fiber is covered with tiny overlapping scales so that the fibers lock together when they are spun into yarn. A merino ram can produce 26 pounds of wool.

WORLD WAR I

World War I (1914–1918) involved Europe, the United States, and much of the Middle East, so it became known as a "world war." France, Britain (and her empire), the United States, and Russia were on one side. On the other were Austria-Hungary, Germany, and Turkey.

The war reached a stalemate in northern France, where the front lines of both sides barely moved for several years. In the east, the Germans fared better. Because of this and its own internal problems, Russia was forced to withdraw from the struggle in 1917.

The United States was at first reluctant to be drawn into the conflict, but after many German attacks on U.S. shipping, the United

States declared war on Germany. The Allied armies slowly pushed the Germans back, until peace was agreed in November 1918.

WORLD WAR II

In September 1939, Adolf Hitler's German armies invaded Poland, an early step in his planned conquest of Europe. Germany, then Italy, and eventually Japan, had entered into a war against most of the major nations of the world. Before the war was over, battles had been fought from the North Atlantic and Europe to the tropical jungles of the Far East.

At first, the Germans were successful in their sweep across Europe, and into North Africa and Russia. In December 1941, the United States entered the war after the Japanese bombed the Pacific Fleet at Pearl Harbor in Hawaii,

and the tide began to turn. By June 1944, Allied forces had landed in France. Germany surrendered the following spring.

In the Pacific, Japan had invaded China, the Malaya Peninsula, and Indonesia, and had captured many Pacific islands. Victories by the U.S. Navy and finally, the dropping of atomic bombs on the Japanese cities of Hiroshima and Nagasaki forced Japan to surrender.

WORM

Worms are animals with soft bodies. Some live underground or in water; others as parasites inside plants or other animals.

There are around 20,000 different kinds of worms. One group includes flatworms, which have flat, ribbon, or leaf-shaped bodies. The harmful parasites, the tapeworm and the liver fluke,

World War I: For four years, fighting centered around two lines of trenches stretching across western Europe.

are flatworms. Threadworms, roundworms, and hookworms belong to another group. Many of these are also parasites.

Segmented worms are not harmful. Their bodies consist of many segments or rings. Tiny bristles on the segments help them to move along. They include ragworms, lugworms, and earthworms. Earthworms live in moist soil, and eat bits of leaves and decayed plant matter in the soil. They come to the surface to feed or after heavy rain. Earthworms help the garden by turning over the soil and breaking it up.

See also PARASITE.

WRIGHT, ORVILLE (1871–1948) AND WILBUR (1867–1912)

These two American brothers made the first motor-powered, heavier-than-air flight in 1903.

They taught themselves about flight by making and flying kites and gliders. By 1903, they were ready to attach a four-cylinder, 13 horsepower engine to a biplane

Wright Brothers: *The world's first successful powered airplane,* Flyer 1, *took to the air in 1903.*

glider. On December 17th, Orville took off, rose to a height of nearly ten feet, and flew more than 100 feet. The flight took 59 seconds.

X-RAY

X-rays were discovered by the German scientist Wilhelm Roentgen in 1895. They are invisible waves of energy like light waves, and can pass through and into most materials. They pass through flesh, for example. In hospitals, doctors take X-ray photographs to look inside the body. A patient stands in front of a photographic film and X-rays are passed through him. When the film is developed, the patient's bones show up. This is because the bones block some of the rays and cast a shadow on the film. The doctors can see if any of the bones are broken. Some new X-ray machines can photograph body organs as well

Y

YAK

Yaks live in the cold, high mountains of Central Asia. The yak can live on the poor pasture of the Himalaya Mountains. It produces milk, butter, and meat, its skin is made into leather, and its long, shaggy hair is woven into cloth.

ZEBRA

The zebra is a relation of the horse. Its distinct black stripes help to camouflage it in the shadowy high grass of the African plains on which it lives. Zebras roam in herds, and gallop off at great speed if attacked by lions, their main enemy.

ZOO

A zoo is a place where wild animals are kept in captivity. People enjoy going to zoos to see animals from other countries. But, more important, zoos help to save rare animals from becoming extinct.

In the past, kings collected wild animals in zoos. The first public zoos started in the 1800s. Often the cages were too small for the animals and the bars made it difficult for people to see them.

Today, many zoos have enclosures in which the animals feel more at home. Ditches, moats, and glass keep the animals and visitors apart. Birds fly around inside large aviaries. Mountain goats climb artificial hills, while penguins, polar bears, seals, and even elephants have pools to splash in. In special darkened buildings, people can see animals that are normally active only at night.

ZOOLOGY

This is the science that deals with the study of animals. Zoologists find out about animals' bodies, their growth patterns, and habits. Around one million different species, or kinds, of animals have been described by zoologists and sorted into groups.

The study of zoology helps us to control animal pests and diseases, and to improve the quality of farm animals.

Yak: The yak's shaggy hair protects it from the cold.

Index

Page numbers in **bold** type denote main entries; page numbers in *italic* type refer to illustrations and charts.